DATE			

UNEMPLOYMENT: ECONOMIC PERSPECTIVES

UNEMPLOYMENT

Economic Perspectives

Guy Routh

First published 1986

Published by
THE MACMILLAN PRESS LTD
Houndmills, Basingstoke, Hampshire RG21 2XS
and London
Companies and representatives
throughout the world

Typeset by Wessex Typesetters
(Division of The Eastern Press Ltd)
Frome, Somerset

Printed in Hong Kong

British Library Cataloguing in Publication Data
Routh, Guy
Unemployment: economic perspectives.
1. Unemployment
I. Title
331.13'7   HD5707.5
ISBN 0–333–41269–9 (hardcover)
ISBN 0–333–41270–2 (paperback)

Contents

List of Tables and Figures

TABLES

The following symbols have been used in the tables:

   . . . = not available
   — = nil or negligible (less than half the final digit shown)
   n.e.c. = not elsewhere classified
   n.e.s. = not elsewhere specified

FIGURES

Preface

Every year, the British Universities Industrial Relations Association (BUIRA) invites one of its members to present a review paper to the ensuing annual conference on a subject agreed by the reviewer and the executive. I was chosen for this task in 1982 and presented my paper in July 1983, its title 'The Industrial Relations of Inflation and Unemployment'. The report on the conference remarked, 'His research objective had been to determine the true relationship between wages, prices and unemployment, but sadly he was to conclude that the relationship remained obscure'. I spent a further two years gathering material and seeking enlightenment in various countries, the result being the book that follows. I am grateful to those members of the BUIRA who answered my questions or explained why they were unanswerable.

I was helped, too, by Dr Robert Ray of the International Institute for Labour Studies in Geneva, and by Dr Guy Standing of the International Labour Office, and extended my knowledge of industrial relations theory by a day of intensive study under the direction of Mr Oliver Clarke at the OECD in Paris.

I feel particular gratitude for many years of aid from Mrs Sheila Schaffer and Mr David Kennelly of the Documents Section of the University of Sussex Library, in obedience to whom statistical tables and government reports spring instantly to hand, however obscure they may be. My wife has assisted in ways that, to borrow Marshall's imagery, 'are not seen', but which control the course of those episodes which 'are seen'. She has listened to and discussed my ideas with fortitude and has read and corrected the typescript and proofs.

While the economic portents remain gloomy, hopes for the understanding of economics have been advanced by the establishment of the Employment Institute and the Charter for Jobs. Their proposals have come under attack but, as Keynes and Hubert Henderson wrote in 1929, 'The objections which are raised are mostly not the objections of experience or of practical men. They are based on highly abstract theories–venerable, academic inventions, half misunderstood by those who are applying them today, and based on assumptions which are contrary to the facts' (Keynes and Henderson, 1929, p. 91).

Brighton   GUY ROUTH

1 Introduction

1.1 THE NATURE OF UNEMPLOYMENT

Unemployment is a familiar affliction of our age, but its nature, causes and cure remain matters of dispute. As with many familiar things, closer examination leads to deepening mystery. Its pathology is complex, with social as well as economic ramifications. Accounts of Paradise make no mention of regular employment but depict a regime of eternal idleness, while in Hell sinners are in a state of full employment, perpetually stoking. So, from one viewpoint, work is painful and to be avoided, and those who are paid for not working should consider themselves fortunate. But from another, work, with its regular routine and activities, forms an essential framework for the personality, giving the worker status and a sense of identity, both within the family and in the outside world. The worker is the provider on whose wages the household depends for its livelihood, and by whose products and services human societies are sustained.

More than half the items entering into household consumption, including food and drink, fuel and light, transport and communication, are required every day, or at least every weekday. To a large extent we live, as it were, from hand to mouth. A continuous flow of goods and services must be maintained for life to be preserved. Some consumer goods are bought occasionally and last a long time, and about a fifth of total resources in the United Kingdom go into 'capital formation', most of it to compensate for capital used up in the course of the year, the rest to add to the buildings and machinery that will increase the flow of products in years to come. Those in employment each play a part in this complex system by which humanity is preserved and renewed, day by day or year by year, according to the length of the relevant cycle of production. Those who are unemployed are bystanders, excluded from participation in this life process, unless they can re-enter *sub rosa* through the black economy.

Alienation and anomie accompany loss of a job and the inability to find one. The routine of the working day establishes a gauge by which

1

other activities can be measured. It gives meaning to rest and recreation, and constant reassurance to the worker of his social importance and orientation:

> work is also one of the most active ways in which the individual is linked to the family group, forming in many cases its indispensable cement without which both the group and the individual become unbalanced and disintegrate. Loss of work, while constituting a social setback for the unemployed person, also produces after a while a 'toxic condition' requiring complete readaptation. (Friedmann, 1961, pp. 128–9)

Full employment was listed high amongst the declarations of intent that accompanied the end of the second world war. In Britain, the White Paper of May 1944 announced, 'The Government accept as one of their primary aims and responsibilities the maintenance of a high and stable level of employment after the war'. In the United States, the Employment Act of 1946 established the President's Council of Economic Advisers and committed the government 'to co-ordinate and utilize all its plans, functions and resources . . . to promote maximum employment and purchasing power'. This aim was extended by the Full Employment and Balanced Growth Act of 1978 which 'establishes as a national goal the fulfilment of the right to full opportunities for useful paid employment at fair rates of compensation of all individuals able, willing, and seeking to work (The President [of the United States], 1979, p. xv).

Yet there is one school of thought that views the growth of unemployment with fortitude. Their influence was asserted in Britain in 1979 and in the United States in 1980, so that the preservation of full employment lapsed as a prime aim of policy, subordinated to control of the quantity and preservation of the value of money. Indeed, there was held to be a 'trade-off' between unemployment and inflation, so that inflation could be restrained by the active promotion of unemployment. Some of the doctrines conveying this idea will be reviewed in Chapter 4. I shall argue, in Chapter 5, that these views are economically wrong as well as morally reprehensible, that unemployment is a social evil on a par with infant mortality, drug addiction, road accidents, illiteracy and crime, and that governments have a moral obligation to combat it.

There are three reasons that may explain the currency in government circles of this perverse doctrine: those with secure jobs terminating in indexed pensions do not appreciate the nature of unemployment. They underrate its awfulness just as men tend to underrate the trauma of child-birth. The second reason is that the issue of unemployment is obscured by a confusion of competing explanations. These will be examined in Chapters 3 and 4. The third is that though 12 or 13 per cent of the labour force is unemployed, less than 6 per cent of *voters* are unemployed, while people in employment are actually better off at the end of 1985 than they were at the beginning of 1979, for average earnings have gone up nearly 20 per cent more than average retail prices.

1.2 NOTE ON METHODOLOGY

I hope that it will be useful at this preliminary stage to insert a note on 'methodology' (the means by which theories are invented, elaborated, presented and judged). Wonder is often expressed at the way in which economists contradict one another. Surely, if their subject is to be of any practical use, they should first meet together and agree on what is wrong and how to put it right? Instead, they dispute with one another, heatedly and in public. On the subject with which we are here concerned:

i.   Keynesians (or Post-Keynesians) argue that unemployment is due to a deficiency of demand for the products of industry, and that this can be remedied by promoting increased expenditure on investment or consumption.

ii.   Monetarists maintain that increased expenditure, of the sort envisaged by the Keynesians, would pass straight through the system in the form of higher prices, and that the prime need is for rigorous control of the money supply.

iii. Proponents of the Phillips curve believe that there is a 'natural rate of unemployment' which, if it were sustained, would eliminate inflation.

iv.   Supply-side economists maintain that production (and thus employment) can be increased by providing a more lavish return to entrepreneurs and reducing income tax.

v.   Some believe that government expenditure is an awful burden on business and that it must be drastically reduced.

vi.   And others that the way forward lies through the further extension of public consumption (of those goods and services, like education, health, sport, music, art and public amenities that are provided through public expenditure for communal enjoyment) by which deficiencies in private consumption may be made up.

vii.   Marxists believe that crisis and instability are built-in features of the capitalist system; that booms and slumps will continue their disruptive sway until people tire of them and transform their societies from capitalism to socialism.

There are combinations and variations of the above ideas that are the subject of particular disputes. One such arose thirty years ago and is still a matter of controversy: whether the inflation with which full employment is associated is the result of cost-push or demand-pull. Those who point to cost-push believe that trade unions are responsible for pushing up costs and prices, and that this process can be restrained by incomes policies or changes in the system of industrial relations. Those who point to demand-pull specify 'too much money chasing too few goods', a process that can be remedied by a restriction of the supply of money. Another controversy is of more recent origin: non-Keynesians have never taken kindly to the idea of involuntary unemployment – that is, that unemployment is not the fault of the unemployed. The 'search' model has now been presented, in terms of which the unemployed are better viewed as people who are sorting through the list of job opportunities in search of one that meets their requirements. How long they will remain unemployed depends on how hard they are to please (see Standing, 1981, p. 564).

The co-existence of these contradictory systems of thought suggests a methodological laxity in university departments of economics, where every teacher is expected to set up as a theorist without any prior requirement of research or experience in the world of business. Indeed, 'pure' theory, highly rated in economic cosmology, means theory uncontaminated by contact with reality. The theorist gains credit by devising an imaginary set of relationships (called a 'model'), expresses them mathematically, and then deduces the path by which they would achieve equilibrium and maximise their product.

In the natural sciences, models are devised as provisional explanations of phenomena whose existence has been established by research; these models are in due course put to the test, refuted and discarded, or confirmed and further developed. In academic economics, by contrast, models are derived from the mind of the modeller and enjoy unlimited existence. They may go out of fashion and be forgotten, only to be revived years, or even centuries, later and exhibited as examples of the prescience of their originators and the sapience of the rediscoverer. They are better described as 'pet theories'. They are now presented with mandatory mathematical camouflage that makes the simple-minded appear abstruse and the absurd ingenious. The PTs reproduce at enormous speed, forced on by their authors' quest for tenure and promotion; they are as numerous as 'instrumental theories' (ITs) are rare. The ITs are designed to achieve some useful purpose (other than tenure or promotion). They derive from empirical studies and are policy-orientated or problem-solving in character. In orthodox academic economics, a theory is a hypothesis in disguise; 'proofs' are offered in the form of heavily-doctored statistics forced into econometric moulds. As Leontief has written, 'the econometricians fit algebraic functions of all possible shapes to essentially the same sets of data without being able to advance, in any perceptible way, a systematic understanding of the structure and the operations of a real economic system' (Eichner, 1983, pp. x–xi). Wassily Leontief is a past president of the American Economic Association and has been awarded the Nobel Prize in Economics.

It is important to remember that you may be quite certain about something, and yet quite wrong. Pet theorists suffer from this disability in respect of their pet theories, and are thus prone to proclaim them as if they were established facts that brooked no denial. So the politician, student or enquiring layman who turns to economics in search of understanding is like Pilgrim in his search for the Shining Gate, beset by endless dangers, with temptations to accept what flatters his prejudices rather than what is true. Hypotheses, models, declarations, theorems, must be critically examined before acceptance. You must ask of their authors, 'How does he know? Does he base his findings on a proper analysis of carefully collected data, or is he exercising a pet theory derived from nothing more substantial than that he happens to like the idea?

1.3 DEFINITIONS

In pre-capitalist times, deprivation was not associated with unemployment, except in over-crowded regions where there was not enough land to go round. It was the result of war, pestilence, drought, flood or other natural disaster. It is a peculiarity of capitalist systems that deprivation accompanies surpluses of unsaleable goods. People are deprived not because there is not enough but because there is too much.

Because the level of unemployment is such an important indicator of the health of the economy, the governments of industrialised countries have elaborate systems of measuring it. In an attempt to standardise practices, the International Conference of Labour Statisticians has agreed that to be classed as unemployed you must be of working age – that is, above the age of compulsory schooling; on the day of the count, you must be without a job, able to work (that is, not ill or 'institutionalised'), and you must be seeking work for pay or profit (International Labour Office, 1959).

In the United Kingdom and most OECD countries, to be included in the monthly count you must be registered at a government employment office. (The 24 countries that are members of the Organisation for Economic Co-operation and Development include the capitalist countries of Europe plus Canada, the United States, Japan, Australia, New Zealand and Turkey.) If you are not so registered you will not be counted, no matter how hard you may be looking for a job. Some of these countries, however, get their data not from employment offices but from monthly surveys in which officials visit a sample of households and question them. Their criterion is not whether or not a person is registered as unemployed, but whether in fact he or she is without a job, able to work and seeking paid employment. Japan, Canada, the United States and Sweden follow such a system. (On the method used in the United States, see Bureau of Labor Statistics, 1966.)

In addition to the monthly count, the EEC countries carry out a labour force survey (LFS) every two years. The British survey in 1984 covered 77 000 households. A smaller General Household Survey (GHS), covering 15 000 households, is made annually in Britain. From these it is possible to check the accuracy of the monthly count, which leaves out people looking for work who have not registered as unemployed, but *includes* those who register who are *not* looking for work. In 1981 it was found that 130 000 unemployed males and 270 000 unemployed females had not registered, so that the monthly count underestimated the number of unemployed by 400 000 in this respect. But curiously enough, the LFS found that the number of unregistered unemployed was balanced by the number of registered unemployed who were not actively seeking work. 'These include some occupational pensioners and others who registered only in order to obtain national insurance credits, some who would welcome a job if the Jobcentre were to offer them a suitable one but are not so concerned as to consider themselves as actively job seeking . . . and some who are virtually unemployable or do not believe that any jobs are available for them' (*Employment Gazette*, June 1983, pp. 265–7). The official statistics include some ambiguous elements, though they are accurate enough for most purposes. Their nature and history are described in Garside, 1980, while Constance Sorrentino reconciles them for various OECD countries in an annual series, 1959 to 1979 (Showler and Sinfield, 1981, p. 170).

1.4 EXTENT OF UNEMPLOYMENT IN THE OECD

The official series on unemployment, then, purport to measure the number of people who are without gainful employment, but actively seeking it. The major difference in method is between governments whose officials interview a sample of households and those who rely on registration at employment offices. Even amongst the latter, methods vary (see the *Employment Gazette*, August 1980, pp. 833–40). When the methods are applied consistently, the resulting series are good for measuring trends within a particular country and adequate for measuring differences between countries. Note, though, that they are not a measure of potential but unused labour resources. There are large numbers of people, particularly married women, who are not 'in the labour market', that is, looking for work, because they see no chance of finding it and there are many who are working below their capacity because of the shortfall of opportunities in the field in which they are qualified. (For a lucid exposition of these problems, see International Institute for Labour Studies, 1984, pp. 5–11.)

Thus warned, let us look at Table 1.1: the percentage of people listed as unemployed in the major OECD countries – that is, the number of job-seekers expressed as a proportion of all employees (employed and unemployed) in each country. In 1974, the

TABLE 1.1 *Percentage of labour force unemployed in various countries (monthly averages 1974 and 1984)*

	Canada	France	German FR	UK	Italy	Japan	Sweden	United States
1974	5.4	2.3	2.6	2.6	4.8	1.4	2.0	5.6
1984	11.3	12.0	9.2	13.2	13.1	2.7	3.2	7.5

SOURCE *Employment Gazette*, August 1980, January and September 1985.

industrialised capitalist world was coming to the end of a 25-year era in which shortage of workers was more of a problem than shortage of jobs. There had been a strong flow of populations from the countryside to the towns, and of 'guest workers' from poor to rich countries. By 1984, conditions had been transformed. Note how circumstances vary between countries. Japan and Sweden remain at the bottom of the unemployment scale, but the United Kingdom, near the bottom in 1974, has now outdone all the rest. In the United Kingdom, unemployment crossed the 5 per cent barrier in 1976 but remained below 6 per cent until 1980. In July 1981, it crossed the 10 per cent mark and, in August 1982, reached 12 per cent.

Of course there is unemployment in 'less developed countries', but of a different kind, due not to the superabundance of everything but to shortages of some important factor or factors of production: skilled labour, capital equipment, know-how or essential raw materials. Their modern industrial establishments can employ only a small fraction of the labour force, even if the flow of raw materials or spare-parts is not held up by shortages of foreign exchange. But in the OECD countries all the required factors of production are present: equipment, buildings, materials, skills and spare capacity in already-established factories. All the elements of the infrastructure are ready to hand. Output could be increased by, say, 15 per cent without much difficulty (see Glyn and Harrison, 1980, p. 171). It is not that appetites are sated, leaving nothing more to be done: more and better clothing and household durables could be usefully employed, old houses could be modernised, new ones built, education expanded, public transport improved. After all, between 1939 and 1940, GDP rose by nearly 15 per cent in the United Kingdom, and there was less spare labour then than in 1984.

The trouble is that we do not have the social and political forces capable of organising such an upsurge: what we can do in war we lack the will to do in peace. So the spare capacity, unemployed labour and surplus raw materials must remain wasted. Fifteen per cent of the United Kingdom's GDP at factor cost in 1983 would have amounted to nearly £30 billion, now lost and gone for ever.

Of course, the wastage of resources by the OECD countries amounts to a great deal more. On average in 1983 there were nearly 12 million unemployed in the EEC, and 14.4 million in the United States, Australia, Canada and Japan. The total is very near the whole working population (including employers and self-employed) of the United Kingdom.

The colossal waste of existing capacity is compounded by the lost opportunities of past years: technical and organisational improvements should be continuously raising output per unit of labour and per unit of capital as well as providing new jobs for those entering the labour force. Even in the troubled sixties the number of employees in employment in the United Kingdom rose on average by 40 000 per year, and industrial production at an annual rate of 2.75 per cent (Department of Employment, 1971, p. 243, and *Annual Abstract of Statistics, 1971*, p. 125). The Index of Industrial Production measures the change in real output in mining, manufacturing, construction, gas, electricity and water.

Between December 1979 and December 1983, by contrast, the seasonally adjusted number of employees in employment fell from 23 244 000 to 20 828 000: an average of 50 000 per month. Between 1979 and 1983, industrial production, instead of rising by 11.5 per cent (2.75 per cent a year), fell by 6 per cent. The loss in the value of industrial production for 1983, on this fairly modest basis, would have been £16 717 million; the cumulative loss at current prices, 1980 to 1983 inclusive, would have been £54 205 million (see Central Statistical Office, 1984, Table 2.2, p. 21, and Table 2.4 p. 23).

If opportunities are missed this year, next year has to start from a lower base: the effect is cumulative. So, too, is the effect of unemployment on the labour force. Schools are supposed to convey to their pupils literacy, numeracy and understanding; professional education can be performed by universities and technical colleges, but the major element of training is done on the job. Even engineers are not much good to their employers until they have spent a few years of training-on-the-job and learning-by-doing. So unemployment at present levels is losing millions of worker-days of possible experience and training that, like lost production, can never be recovered.

1.5 DIMENSIONS OF UNEMPLOYMENT IN THE UNITED KINGDOM

1.5.1 **By Occupation**

We seek to learn more about unemployment by analysing it in various ways: by occupation, industry, region, age, sex and duration. By experience and/or training, workers are qualified to do certain jobs. For purposes of classification, jobs are grouped in particular occupations, and different occupations are afflicted by unemployment to varying degrees. Workers may change the industry in which they perform their occupation or they may be retrained or otherwise seek qualifications to enable them to change their occupation. But once people have settled into a particular occupation, a decision to change to another is quite a serious one.

The most exhaustive survey of the occupational distribution of the working population is made in the decennial Census of Population. Some hundreds of occupations are distinguished, each allocated to one of seventeen classes. For each occupation and for each class we are told how many people were in employment and how many were unemployed at the time of the Census. In Table 1.2, the seventeen classes have been reduced to thirteen, and employment and unemployment in each shown as a percentage of total employment and unemployment.

In April 1981 there were 2 489 400 unemployed out of a labour force totalling 25 405 590. If unemployment were distributed evenly amongst all the classes, then each would have a share of

TABLE 1.2   *Employment and unemployment by occupational class Great Britain, 1981*

	In employment %	Unemployed %
Professional and related	17.7	5.2
Managerial	9.8	3.4
Clerical and related	16.9	6.5
Selling	6.0	3.4
Security and protective service	2.3	1.1
Catering, cleaning, personal service	10.7	5.8
Farming, fishing and related	1.5	1.3
Materials processing, making and repairing	18.8	18.9
Painting, repetitive assembling, packaging and related	3.8	4.9
Construction, mining and related	3.4	6.9
Transport, storing and related	6.4	7.5
Miscellaneous	1.8	4.8
Inadequately described and not stated	0.9	30.2
	100.0	100.0

SOURCE   Office of Population Censuses and Surveys, Registrar General Scotland, *Census 1981, Economic Activity Great Britain* (HMSO, 1984)

unemployment equal to its share of employment. In every hundred employed, 17.7 were professional and related. But amongst the unemployed, only 5.2 per hundred were professional and related, less than ⅓ of the 'expected' proportion. As you go down the table, you will note that the proportion unemployed rises gradually until, for those engaged in materials processing, making and repairing, the proportion unemployed is just about equal to the proportion employed. In construction, mining and related, unemployment is double the 'expected' value, for 'miscellaneous' 2⅔ times, and for 'inadequately described and not stated' more than 30 times.

One can look at the data from a different perspective by asking, 'What percentage of each occupational class was unemployed?' The Census shows that 9.8 per cent of the labour force were unemployed. But in the case of professional and related, only 3.1 per cent were unemployed. Of the managers, 3.6 per cent were unemployed, of the clerical and related, 4.0 per cent.

But when we reach the processors, makers and repairers, unemployment is at the national average: 9.8 per cent. For the remaining groups, it is well above the average. Of those whose occupation was inadequately described or not stated, 78.6 per cent were unemployed.

There are also contrasts within each of these broad groups. Amongst the professionals and related, those in science, engineering and technology were a bit above the average at 3.6 per cent, but in literary, artistic and sporting pursuits, 8.25 per cent were unemployed.

Rates amongst skilled manual workers vary about the national average, but with compositors particularly low (3.8 per cent) and bricklayers particularly high (18.4 per cent).

But these rates are insignificant compared with those amongst unskilled workers, that include the bulk of those whose occupation was inadequately described or not stated. Of these, rates of unemployment were as follows:

	%
Building and civil engineering labourers	35.4
General labourers	23.5
Inadequately described and not stated	56.6
All the above	38.0

At the time of the onset of the depression of the early thirties, unemployment was also excessively high amongst the unskilled. The

1931 census showed an overall rate of 13.3 per cent for men and 8.9 per cent for women, but for labourers:

		%
Building labourers		19.3
Dock labourers		21.2
Other labourers	Male	32.0
	Female	22.9

For 1951, too, the census showed unemployment for labourers to be about double that for all workers: but the overall rate was only 2.2 per cent for men and 2.0 per cent for women.

Conventional economic theory has it that if anything is in excess supply, its price (or at least its relative price) will fall. This has not been the case with unskilled workers whose relative pay has actually risen over the last 65 years (see Routh, 1980, p. 124).

1.5.2 Unemployment by Industry

Job defines occupation; product defines industry. The changes in the numbers employed in various industries reflect changes in the sales of their products (which may be goods or services), combined with changes in technology and output per worker. Table 1.3 shows changes in employment in various industries, comparing June 1979 with May (or in some cases, March) 1984. The industries consist of Divisions from the Standard Industrial Classification 1980 (Central Statistical Office, 1979), some of which have been further divided by Classes.

There is a brisk turnover of labour always in operation, with workers changing employers and employers changing workers. In four weeks in March 1984, for instance, engagements in manufacturing industry in Britain amounted to 1.5 per cent of the workforce, while those who left amounted to 1.7 per cent (*Employment Gazette*, July 1984, p. S17). But the third column of Table 1.3 shows the number of jobs that have been eliminated in the five years between 1979 (before the advent of the slump) and 1984, or, in a few instances, that have been added.

Employment in three of the groups stood at two-thirds of its 1979 level:

Metal manufacture (mainly iron and steel)
Motor vehicles and parts (cars and commercial vehicles)
Textiles, leather, footwear, clothing.

TABLE 1.3 *Employees by industry, Great Britain, June 1979 and May 1984*

Industry	1979	1984	Differ-ence	84 as % of 79
		Thousands		
Agriculture, forestry, fishing	359	333*	26	93
Coal, oil, natural gas	356	297	59	83
Gas, electricity, water supply	356	337	19	95
Metal manufacture and extraction	683	454	229	66
Chemicals, man-made fibres	427	344	83	81
Mechanical engineering	1011	778	233	77
Office machinery, electrical engineering, instruments	946	835	111	88
Motor vehicles and parts	433	293	140	68
Other transport equipment	432	301	131	70
Metal goods n.e.s.	516	383	133	74
Food, drink, tobacco	715	609	106	85
Textiles, leather, footwear, clothing	809	533	276	66
Timber, wood furniture, rubber, plastics	595	451	144	76
Paper products, printing, publishing	547	485	62	89
Construction	1216	982	234	81
Distributive trades and repairs	3235	3251*	+16	100
Hotels and catering	938	916*	22	98
Transport	1039	876*	63	84
Posts, telecommunications	413	421*	+8	102
Banking, finance, insurance	1638	1854*	+216	113
Public administration	1947	1841*	106	95
Education	1591	1564*	27	98
Health and veterinary services	1186	1292*	+106	109
Other services	1251	1319*	+68	105
All employees	22639	20750*	1889	92

* March 1984.
SOURCE *Employment Gazette*, July 1984, vol. 92, no. 7, pp. S11–12.

Even 'office machinery, electrical engineering and instruments', that should include the most rapidly expanding sections, has shed 111 000 workers. Here included are data processing equipment, electronics and telecommunications, and surgical equipment, that one would hope would absorb the losses from less science-based activities. Construction has discarded 234 000 jobs despite national inadequacies of roads and houses.

On the credit side, wholesale distribution and repairs gained 58 000 jobs, though 42 000 were lost in retailing, leaving a net gain for the order of 16 000. 'Other services' took on 68 000 additional workers. This group includes research and development institutes, churches, trade unions, television, libraries, sport, laundries and hairdressers and personal services n.e.s. But the biggest gain has been in insurance, banking and finance. Money-shops are springing up all over the place as trades disappear; building societies proliferate. We live not by taking in each other's washing, but by lending and borrowing each other's money.

In Chapter 2 we shall try to distinguish between those industries that are in decline and will never recover, those that are merely suffering from the downturn of the trade cycle, and those that are flourishing and shedding workers through technological advances.

1.5.3 Unemployment by Region

Jarrow has gone down into history as 'the town that was murdered'. This is how it was described by Ellen Wilkinson, MP for Jarrow in the 1930s, in her biography of Jarrow published in 1939. 'Jarrow in that year, 1932–33, was utterly stagnant. There was no work. No one had a job, except a few railwaymen, officials, the workers in the co-operative stores, and the few clerks and craftsmen who went out of the town to their jobs each day. The unemployment rate was over 80 per cent' (Wilkinson, 1939, pp. 191–2). The town's people, Labour and Conservative, united in sending the deputation of two hundred citizens on the march to London that so poignantly demonstrated their plight.

There were other towns that suffered as much. Over the whole of the United Kingdom, in 1931 and 1932, one worker in five was unemployed, but the incidence varied greatly from place to place. These differences persist over long periods. Administrators have despaired of persuading people to move so as to even things out for, as Adam Smith remarked, 'a man is of all sorts of luggage the most difficult to be transported'. The extent of regional differences in the middle of 1984 is shown in Table 1.4.

In Greater London, East Anglia and the South West, about one worker in ten had no job; in Northern Ireland one in five. The rates in Northern Ireland are reminiscent of the worst years of the 1930s. In the West Midlands, England's industrial heartland, one worker in seven is without a job.

TABLE 1.4   *Unemployment by region, United Kingdom,*
June 14, 1984

Region	Nos Thousands	%
South East	716.6	9.2
inc. Greater London	369.6	9.7
East Anglia	73.1	9.6
South West	179.3	10.6
North	223.9	17.6
Wales	162.9	15.2
Scotland	329.1	14.6
Northern Ireland	118.9	20.5
West Midlands	335.1	14.7
East Midlands	185.6	11.6
Yorkshire and Humberside	280.1	13.7
North West	425.1	15.4

SOURCE   *Employment Gazette*, July 1984, pp. S28–30.

Between the areas into which the regions are divided, the range is still higher. There are a few places with less than 5 per cent unemployed, but a number with more than 20 per cent. In Northern Ireland, in June 1984, Cookstown has 35.3 per cent unemployed, and Strabane 40.3 (*Employment Gazette*, July 1984, pp. S31–33).

Why are there these great contrasts between different places? Part of the explanation is contained in Table 1.3. The fact that an area was heavily committed to metal manufacture, shipbuilding, vehicles, textiles or clothing would itself have ensured that it lost 20 per cent or more of its jobs between 1979 and 1984. If, like the City of London, it were dedicated to money matters, employment would have risen comfortably.

But this does not explain why a company wishing to establish a new factory should not take advantage of the abundance of labour where it is available. But there are many factors that are taken into consideration: the convenience and salubriousness of the place, the availability of housing for company employees who are transferred, the skills locally available amongst the unemployed and, of considerable moment, the grants and subsidies that local authorities or central governments are willing to pay. There are tax exemptions and special allowances available for firms willing to invest in what used to be called depressed areas, but are now more delicately referred to as 'assisted areas'. European governments are willing to negotiate special treaties with the multinationals to induce them to open plants in their countries, as the British government has done with Nissan to whom grants may reach £100 million by the end of the present decade. £80 million was wagered (and lost) on DeLorean.

1.5.4   Unemployment by Age and Sex

I have already referred to the way in which the official series on unemployment over or under-state the number of unemployed. The variations differ for men and women. In the *Employment Gazette* for June 1983 (pp. 265–7) the monthly count of unemployed is compared with the findings of the 1981 Labour Force Survey and the General Household Survey.

The monthly count, you may remember, is of those who are registered at Job Centres as seeking employment. The average for Great Britain in 1981 was:

Women 649 000
Men 1 773 000.

But the interviews conducted for the Labour Force and General Household Surveys suggested the need for the following corrections:

Registered, but not seeking work:
    women, 156 000; men, 248 000
Seeking work, but not registered:
    Women, 270 000; men, 130 000.

The true number of women unemployed would thus be 649 000 + 114 000 (an addition of 18 per cent), and of men 1 773 000 − 118 000 (a reduction of 7 per cent).

If we apply these adjustments to the numbers of females and males returned as unemployed in 1983 (averaging the monthly counts for that year) the rate for females is increased from 8.7 to 10.3 per cent, and for males reduced from 15.6 to 14.5 per cent. The rate for men remains appreciably worse.

The over-statement is more particularly for older men who have to all intents and purposes retired though they have not yet reached the age of 65. They are receiving unemployment pay and are credited with National Insurance contributions (thus slightly raising their pensions) but are not really seeking work. The under-statement in the case of the women relates particularly to married women with children at school, who would like to find a job but for whom there is no purpose in

registration. It is this that will have contributed to the widening gap
between men and women illustrated in Table 1.5. In the first two age
groups, the rate for men is higher than that for women by 15 and 16 per
cent respectively (I am expressing the one rate as a percentage of the
other). In the age group 20–24, it is 32 per cent higher. After age 35,
the men's rate becomes, and remains, more than double that for
women.

TABLE 1.5   *Unemployment by sex and age, United Kingdom,
October 1983*

	Percentages of relevant age-group unemployed							
Age:	*Under 18*	*18–19*	*20–24*	*25–34*	*35–44*	*45–54*	*55–59*	*60 & over*	*All ages*
Men	28.7	27.9	21.7	13.7	11.4	10.8	14.5	20.5	16.3
Women	24.9	24.0	16.4	9.5	4.4	4.9	6.9	0.1	9.7

SOURCE   *Employment Gazette*, December 1983, p. S36.

But even with the correction for understatement, the women are in a
more favourable position *vis-à-vis* unemployment than the men.
Again, Table 1.3 offers an explanation. Women's employment
happens to be concentrated in industries where the labour force has
expanded or fallen only moderately:

	Employment 1984 as % of 1979	*% of female employment 1984*
Distributive trades, hotels, catering	100	24.8
Banking, finance, insurance	113	9.9
Public administration	95	7.8
Education	98	11.6
Health	109	11.3
Other services	105	5.2
		70.6

(Female employment: March 1984. *Employment Gazette*, July 1984,
pp. S15–16.)

During and after the second world war there was a great demand for
young workers. Large numbers were used as cheap labour for
dead-end jobs, but employers were eager, too, to take them in and
train them for administrative, skilled and semi-skilled jobs. In the
1960s, boys and girls under 18 constituted only a little over 4 per cent of
the unemployed. In 1983, they formed double the proportion of a total

that had been multiplied by a factor of more than six. In November 1960, there were 15 000 of them unemployed; in October 1983, there were 243 000, despite the increase in the numbers staying in full-time education.

The daunting levels of unemployment shown in Table 1.5 do not begin abating until people are in their twenties. The longer the depression endures, the larger the proportion becomes of those who have had no work training nor acquired useful experience.

1.5.5 Unemployment by Duration

The unemployed are not a static group, for workers are constantly moving into or out of employment: labour turnover in manufacturing is about 25 per cent per year. In the quarter ended 14 July 1983, 672 000 males and 360 500 females entered the unemployment register, while 834 000 males and 349 000 females left, some of them, of course, on retirement. A surprising number leave voluntarily (in the United States the statistics distinguish between 'quits' and 'layoffs') because they do not get on with the boss, because the monotony of a particular job has become unbearable, to go to a better job or for many other reasons.

TABLE 1.6   *Numbers unemployed by time unemployed and sex, UK October 1983*

	One week or less	Over 1 –8	Over 8 –52	Over 52 –156	Over 156	All
					Nos. in thousands	
Males	58.0	380.9	826.7	654.9	241.9	2162.4
Females	31.6	235.0	418.9	198.5	47.6	931.6
All	89.6	615.9	1245.6	853.4	289.5	3094.0
% of total	2.9	19.9	40.3	27.6	9.4	100

SOURCE   *Employment Gazette*, December 1983, p. S31.

In Table 1.6, those unemployed in October 1983 are classified by the length of time for which they had been unemployed. The median period for men was 39 or 40 weeks, for women just over 26 weeks.

But what is most disquieting is the accumulation of unemployed who have been without a job for a year or more:

January 1982: 717 000 males (32.5 per cent);
188 000 females (21.7 per cent)

April 1984: 948 500 males (43.5 per cent);
270 000 females (29.1 per cent).

(Employment Gazette, July 1984, p. S36)

The chances of finding a new job diminish with length of unemployment; the black economy offers the only hope of salvation.

1.6 VARIETIES OF UNEMPLOYMENT

We have looked at unemployment from various angles and measured the facets that are thus exposed. Some workers are unemployed for personal reasons: whatever the state of business, they drift from job to job or become 'unemployable'. They are the concern of social workers rather than economists. But other types of unemployment take the form of epidemics that affect occupations, industries, regions or the world. In Chapter 3 we shall examine how these have been analysed by economists, and the various explanatory hypotheses and theories that they have advanced.

Until the publication of Keynes's *General Theory of Employment, Interest and Money* in 1936, orthodox economists argued that all unemployment was voluntary, unless occasioned by sickness, accident or old age. An unemployed worker could always get a job by moving to an area where jobs were available and/or by reducing the wage demanded to whatever employers are willing to pay. Keynes argued by contrast that in the case of *cyclical unemployment*, in which a recession or depression was caused by a deficiency of demand for the products of industry, a general reduction of wages would further reduce demand, while prices would follow the reduction of costs so that *real* wages (wages measured in terms of what they can buy) would remain unchanged.

In Chapter 2, we shall trace the course of the trade cycle over the years, demonstrating the curious rise and fall of business activity that communicates itself from country to country in a rhythm for which various explanations have been offered.

Cyclical fluctuations are the most challenging and the most devastating, for they occur on a world scale and are lavishly wasteful of resources. There are, too, *seasonal fluctuations* that are conspicuous enough to have been long recognised. They apply particularly to agriculture and the tourist trade and its dependencies.

More serious and more intractable is *structural unemployment* occasioned by obsolete elements in the occupational or industrial resources of a country or region. The industrial structure of most European countries and of the United States is faulty in respect of their once-great steel, ship building and textile industries that have suffered permanent damage by competition from Japan, Taiwan and other Asian countries.

The occupational structure of the labour force in the United Kingdom is faulty in that it has far too high an element of unskilled and low-skilled labour. Unemployment in an occupation may be due to the decline of the industry with which it is mainly associated or it may be *technological unemployment*: the industry in question may be thriving but a change in techniques of production may have left certain occupational categories high and dry. Robots replace assembly-line workers; word-processors shorthand-typists or compositors.

Regional unemployment is a combination of factors that emerges when a particular industry has been localised and then suffers from structural decline. This may result in a general deterioration in the area that makes it unattractive for new investment. *Frictional unemployment* is said to occur when job vacancies coexist with unemployment, because the unemployed workers do not have the right skills or are not in the right place.

These are categories of unemployment that most theorists would recognise. There are other varieties in addition to these, associated with some of the arcane theories that we shall meet later on. While taxonomy does not excite the passions, the ascription of causes and prescription of remedies do, especially when the matter in question is the power of trade unions or the supply of money, and thus has political implications.

2 Historical Development

2.1 UNEMPLOYMENT AND THE ORIGINS OF CAPITALISM

Unemployment, in the sense in which we are using it, means being deprived of a job, a would-be employee in search of an employer. A slave cannot be unemployed, though he can be idle if he is given no work to do or if he can avoid it; nor can a serf, for his obligations are laid down by custom.

Thus in ancient times, though beggars and the poor were a familiar feature, they were recognised as such rather than as would-be employees. That the relationship of employer and employee was well-established is illustrated by the householder in Matthew 20, 1 to 16, who went out early in the morning to hire labourers to work in his vineyard, which they agreed to do at a penny a day. Even in predominantly subsistence agricultural areas of Africa there are people who live by hiring out their labour, and Thomas Aquinas (1225–74) thought them important enough to devote part of his *Summa Theologica* to laying down rules as to how they should be paid (Fogarty, 1975, pp. 281–2). John A. Garraty, in his study of unemployment in history writes, 'If unemployment was relatively insignificant in classical times it was, if possible, even less important in the life of the Middle Ages; the condition remained literally inconceivable in the sense, already mentioned, that the term itself did not exist, and also in the sense that it was difficult for a person of the period to envisage a situation in which large numbers of willing and able workers had nothing to do' (Garraty, 1978, p. 15). Work in feudal societies, whether in Europe or Asia, was predetermined by caste, tradition and obligation.

But the plague that swept through Europe between 1347 and 1350 immensely quickened the rate of feudal disintegration. 'The amount of movement, the rapidity of change, the precariousness of life seemed all without precedent. Able-bodied vagrants crowded the roads. Armed bands roamed the countryside. There were beggars everywhere. How to tell an honest artisan trudging to a nearby town in search of work from a renegade soldier or an ordinary tramp, a displaced tenant from a runaway serf, a mendicant monk from a sturdy beggar became increasingly difficult' (Garraty, 1978, p. 20). It was these rambling beggars who formed the nucleus of what was to become 'the reserve army of the unemployed'. But the immediate aim of the legislators was to keep them in one place. The Statute of Labourers required all persons able to labour and without other means of support to remain within their parishes and serve any master at the rates customary prior to the pestilence. Gifts were prohibited to able-bodied beggars who 'refuse to labour, giving themselves to idleness and vice so that they may be, through want, compelled to labour for their necessary living' (Sidney and Beatrice Webb, 1927, p. 25).

The impotence of the law is demonstrated by its increasing severity. An Act of 1536 prescribed that a beggar who refused to go home and stay there should, on the third offence, 'be indicted for wandering, loitering, and idleness, and if convicted, shall suffer execution of death as a felon and an enemy of the commonwealth' (Royal Commission, 1834, pp. 6–13). When, in 1547, this Act was repealed, its failure was ascribed to 'the foolish pitie and mercie of those who should have seen the said godly lawes executed, and partly owing to the perverse nature and long accustomed idleness of the persons given to loytering'.

The severance of feudal obligations occasioned by the Black Death and consolidated by the peasants' revolt was a prerequisite for the hordes of workless beggars that characterised later centuries. The immediate causes were short and sharp, but the effects were worked out over centuries and become discernible only when viewed by an historian's foreshortened gaze. We may see three elements at work, each promoting and being promoted by the others: the renunciation of peasant obligations; supported by the enclosure movement; that was made profitable by the rise of the wool trade.

> when it was realized that enough labour could not be obtained at the old rates, and that no statutes, however severe, could alter the facts of the case, the landlords began to try something new. . . If . . . the land could be farmed on a different plan, a plan in which less labour was required, the difficulty would be at an end. When it was perceived that this could be done by substituting pasture for tillage, and keeping large flocks of sheep which could be conveniently tended by a few shepherds, it was only natural that sheep-farming should spread rapidly. It was doubly profitable; it enabled the

landlord to do without the cultivator who was hard to get, who, if he was a villein, required constant watch to prevent his escape, or if free, demanded wages which seemed exorbitantly high; while, secondly, the increased demand for English wool, caused by the growing prosperity of the native cloth manufacture, raised the price, and rendered sheep-farming more profitable than agriculture even under favourable conditions. (Warner, 1924, pp. 114–15)

The transformation was cumulative but slow and unevenly distributed in time and place. From 1604 to 1914 it was promoted in England by acts of parliament, in terms of which 6.8 million acres were enclosed: 21 per cent of the surface area of England. It is interesting to note that nearly four-fifths of these acts were compressed into the period 1750 to 1819, the resulting rural exodus providing a source of labour for the factories of the industrial revolution (Turner, 1980, p. 32).

We see the destitute as helpless victims of a grand drama of social change, and glimmerings of this view began gradually to appear. In 1516, Sir Thomas More wrote, 'Neither is any punishment so horrible that it can keep them from stealing which have no other craft whereby to get their living', and in the course of the 16th century there is evidence of the acceptance by the legislature of the important principle that, if the able-bodied were to be persuaded to work, work might have to be provided. The penalties for infringement of the law remained fearful, but funds were extracted from parishioners for the relief of the destitute and for the provision of employment for 'sturdy vagabonds'. 'The upgrowth of a great body of people continually in a state of destitution, coincided generally with the creation of a numerous class depending for a livelihood entirely on being hired for day-labour at wages' (Sidney and Beatrice Webb, 1927, p. 43).

Other ingredients were present whose combination was going to lead to the advent of capitalism. Outbreaks of plague that continued to afflict Europe until the 17th century disrupted trade between Europe and Asia, an effect reinforced by the rise of the Ottoman Empire and the vendetta between Christians and Muslims. This inspired and, in due course, financed the great explorations of the 15th and 16th centuries (Parry, 1968, pp. 1–5). There was no difficulty in finding a market for foreign goods imported into Britain; the problem was to find British exports with which to pay for them. At first, raw wool constituted the principal export; in the 16th century this was replaced by woollen cloth. Spinning and weaving developed as a cottage industry, by which rural families augmented their farm incomes. Some historians have designated this 'proto-industrialisation' and claimed it as a phase essential to the development of capitalism. 'Proto-industry occurred in the countryside among peasant farmers and semi-proletarianised workers in need of an income supplement. It was however controlled by urban capital, which integrated it into a new set of regional, supra-regional and international markets. The goods produced were mainly textiles with their mass market potential, but industrial activities included gloving, straw-plaiting, glass-making, leather and metal working' (Houston and Snell, 1984, p. 473. See also Coleman, 1983).

In the years 1473–7, shortcloths exported from the principal English ports amounted to 37 000 (a shortcloth was the standard of measurement applied by the customs authorities to textile exports). By the middle of the 16th century, this had risen to 126 000 (Davis, 1973, p. 52). It was not until the last quarter of the 18th century that the manufacture of cotton textiles became important. By 1802, the value of cotton exports had overtaken that of wool. Between 1802 and 1829 exports of wool textiles hardly changed, while the value of cotton exports increased five-fold (Mitchell and Deane, 1962, p. 295).

As the new society painfully rose from the ruins of the old the authorities continued to treat the casualties of the change with a combination of charity and terror. An Act of 1536 made the support of the impotent poor compulsory for the parishes in which they lived, but if anyone able to work declined to do so, the master whose offer he had refused might enslave him for two years, and 'was directed to feed his slave with bread and water or small drink and such refuse meat as he should think proper; and to cause his slave to work, by beating, chaining, or otherwise in such work and labour (how vile so ever it be) as he should put him unto' (Eden, 1797, Rogers ed., p. 10).

The laws appear to have been the product of impotent rage; more humane people recommended that useful pursuits should be found for those who lacked employment. Sir William Petty guessed that about 100 men in every thousand were without employment (Petty, 1662, p. 32), Gregory King held that of a population of 5½ million in 1696, 1 300 000 were 'cottagers and paupers' and a further 30 000 vagrants (Wilson, 1965, p. 239). In return for a cottage, cottagers would give occasional help to the farmer. 'During a great part of the year he has little or no occasion for their labour, and the cultivation of their own little possession is not sufficient to occupy the time which is left at their own disposal' (Smith, 1776, p. 133).

The army of the unemployed received substantial reinforcements at the time of the industrial revolution by an unprecedented surge in population. The rate of natural increase (births minus deaths as a percentage of total population) had averaged a little over 1 per cent a year in the first half of the 18th century; for 1751–80, it rose to nearly 7 per cent, 1781–1800 nearly 10 per cent, and 1801–1830, just over 14 per cent (Dean and Cole, 1969, p. 115). These rates are derived from averages for the counties of England and Wales. The first census of population was not taken until 1801. Deane and Cole comment, 'And when the full story comes to be told, it may appear that at each stage in the process, the growth of population, itself produced by economic changes in the generation before, was one of the factors which drove the British economy upwards on the path of sustained growth' (ibid. p. 135).

André Armengaud notes that this surge of population was common to European countries, and suggests as causes the fall in the 'crisis death-rate' (that caused by famines, epidemics and wars), followed by a decline in the ordinary death-rate. Improved agricultural productivity resulted in a better fed population, more resistant to disease. This was accompanied by notable advances in medicine (Armengaud, 1970, pp. 25–6).

How are we to classify this mass of workless or under-occupied people present at the birth of the industrial revolution? The difficulty is that our definitions apply to fluctuations and changes in industrial countries whose economies are already 'going concerns', while the Britain of the 17th and 18th centuries was more akin to the poor countries of Africa and Asia than to the Britain of today. By present definitions, most of the cottagers, vagrants and beggars of earlier times would not be classified as unemployed: they were not seeking jobs, because there were no jobs to be sought. As the authors of the employment report on Kenya remarked, 'Applying the concept of unemployment to a poor country is fraught with difficulty' (ILO, 1972, p. 55).

Other similarities suggest themselves. A necessary condition for the emergence of a proletariat was that the labour force should be free of customary rights and obligations. In traditional Africa, missionaries and traders were disconcerted by the refusal of tribespeople to abandon their tribal ways and accept paid employment in road or rail building, plantations and mines. It was only when they were dispossessed of their land or subjected to taxes and other forms of compulsion that they were incorporated in the imperial economy. Then, like the spinners and weavers of proto-industrialism, subsistence incomes were subsidised by wage-labour and wage-labour by subsistence incomes so that neither, by itself, was sufficient to sustain life.

As capitalism developed, unemployment assumed its modern forms, and it is to these that we now turn.

2.2   THE TRADE CYCLE

I have presented the data so as to suggest that the emergence of the factory system was assisted by the existence of reserves of labour. To what extent it was assisted is impossible to say. Marx, as we shall see in Chapter 3, regarded a 'disposable industrial reserve army' as being itself the product of modern industry, increasing and diminishing in phase with the trade cycle. 'As the heavenly bodies, once thrown into a certain definite motion, always repeat this, so is it with social production as soon as it is once thrown into this movement of alternate expansion and contraction' (Marx, 1887, vol. I, pp. 632–3). In this section, we examine the incidence and magnitude of trade or business cycles; in Chapter 3 the theories that have been devised to explain them.

Despite the term 'cycle', that suggests a regular recurrence or repetition, trade cycles have in fact been irregular in timing and extent. Of the four phases that may be distinguished, prosperity, boom, crisis (or slump), and depression, all have varied in length and severity.

They were not the product of the factory system, for they pre-date it, but, with the establishment of an urban proletariat, fluctuations in employment became a conspicuous element in their operation.

Unfortunately, economic thought on the subject was obscured and mystified by the doctrines of Ricardo and J. B. Say who, in the 1820s, denied that there could be such a thing as general over-production. All that was necessary for trade to flourish was that everyone should make the things that everyone else wanted. This became an article of faith in bourgeois economics, its exposition compulsory in lecture courses and textbooks. It was not so difficult for economists to believe as other people might imagine, because it is in keeping with their idea of equilibrium to which economic forces constantly tend and at which output and utility are maximised (Routh, 1975, pp. 134–48). It was not until 1936 that the spell was broken when Keynes presented a formula no less arcane but now confirming reality instead of denying its existence.

It is interesting to note that the phenomena of the trade cycle have been present from at least the closing years of the 17th century, with periods of prosperity interrupted by crisis and depression. 'The *state of confidence*,' Keynes wrote, 'is a matter to which practical men always pay the closest and most anxious attention' (Keynes, 1936, p. 148). The word 'credit' was used to describe the same thing by Charles D'Avenant (1656–1714), Commissioner of Excise and Inspector General of Imports and Exports. 'Of all beings that have existence only in the minds of men, nothing is more fantastical and nice than Credit; it is never to be forced; it comes many times unsought for, and often goes away without reason; and when once lost, is hardly to be quite recovered' (D'Avenant, 1698, p. 151). Boisguillebert, writing in France about the same time, gives a description that fits equally the crises of the modern age. 'The poor are the first to suffer, but the effect communicates itself imperceptibly to the other members of the state, even to the most exalted' (Routh, 1975, pp. 57–9). Sismondi, in 1819, gave a forceful and circumstantial description of the slump that followed the Napoleonic wars, when there could be seen on every side 'proofs of the superabundant production which exceeds consumption' (Routh, 1975, p. 144). Ricardo and Say were beside themselves at the absurdity of this proposition.

For the purposes of this study, trade cycles are of interest because, in their depressive stage they give rise to mass unemployment, but as they move from mania to depression and back again many other interesting features appear that we must not neglect. They can be set off or disturbed by external events: wars, revolutions, crop failures. 'But it is of great importance to point out that our industrial organisation is liable not only to irregular external accidents, but likewise to regular internal changes; that these changes make our credit system much more delicate at some times than at others; and that it is the recurrence of these periodical seasons of delicacy which has given rise to the notion that panics come according to a fixed rule – that every ten years or so we must have one of them' (Bagehot, 1873, p. 123). So depression is often anticipated by financial pyrotechnics: bank failures, stock-market collapse, insolvencies.

There are a number of economic indicators that measure the severity of the fluctuations. The earliest continuous series is for English overseas trade and goes back to 1697. Over the 18th century one can discern nine peaks and seven troughs, with external disturbances from the War of the Spanish Succession (1702–13), and the American War of Independence (1775–81) (Deane and Cole,

1969, p. 49). I present this merely to show that it was operative in that century; I shall not elaborate.

For the 19th century, statistics are more abundant; indeed, Beveridge was able to go back to 1785 for the construction of his index of industrial activity. Like the more recent Index of Industrial Production, it measures changes in the real output of various industries: yards of cloth, tons of cement and so on. The indexes are then weighted together in accordance with some measure of the importance of each industry – in this case the labour employed (Beveridge, 1960, Appendix A). Figure 2.1 depicts the movements in industrial activity between 1785 and 1913. There was a strong upward trend in output over this period, but this has been removed in Beveridge's index, whose aim is to measure fluctuations and not secular (long-term) growth. The economy is shown to have been given a rough ride, not what one would have expected of a divinely-inspired invisible hand maximising by marginal adjustments. Beveridge continues his series to 1938, leaving out the years of the First World War (Beveridge, 1960, pp. 310–13).

There were 19 periods totalling 71 years in which output was below average, and 20 periods totalling 74 years in which it was above average. But the length of each period varies considerably. The median length is 8 years (from the beginning of the above-average to the end of the below-average period) and the range is from 3 to 14 years. The average length of the cycle for the years 1785 to 1859 is 9.25 years, and for the years 1860 to 1938, 6.2 years.

You will observe from the diagram that there was typically a difference of 20 percentage points between troughs and peaks. Between the years of prosperity and depression in each cycle there was, on average, a difference of 14 per cent; it could be as low as 5 per cent and as high as 36 per cent.

These statistics warn us of the unpredictable manic-depressive nature of the economic system. Employment would have fluctuated in response to output, but how closely it is impossible to say. We have a series going back to 1856 showing the rate of unemployment for members of trade unions who operated unemployment benefit funds and who supplied monthly returns to the Board of Trade (Beveridge, 1960, pp. 312–13). They were very select groups of skilled craftsmen.

Agriculture, coal mining, railways, women and unskilled workers hardly affected the series. In mid-1881, the membership of unions reporting regularly was 140 000; in 1901 it was 531 000; and in 1914,

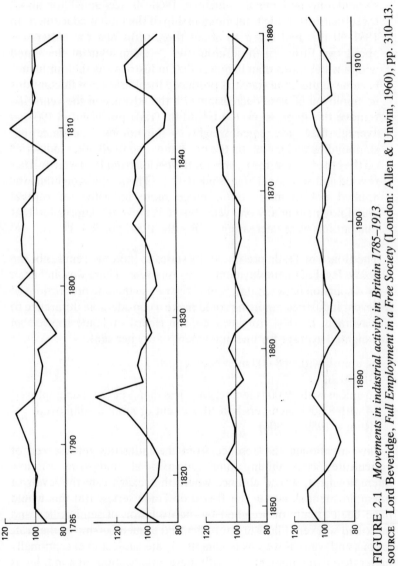

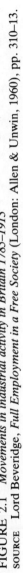

FIGURE 2.1 *Movements in industrial activity in Britain 1785–1913*

SOURCE Lord Beveridge, *Full Employment in a Free Society* (London: Allen & Unwin, 1960), pp. 310–13.

nearly a million. . . One bias was the heavy, though relatively declining, representation of membership in engineering, shipbuilding and metal, which in 1860–70 accounted for about three-quarters of the total membership of the unions concerned. In 1881–90 this had fallen to about three-fifths and thereafter was about two fifths. In these industries . . . employment fluctuated within wider limits than in most other industries. As their influence became diluted, the statistics produced the illusion that fluctuations in employment were decreasing with the advance of the years. To remove this impression, the Board of Trade published in 1904 an average that gave equal weight to the unions in engineering, shipbuilding and metal, on the one hand, and to all other industries on the other. Later, the figures for the period from 1894 were further revised and additional unions inluded. . . This simple weighting was applied not to make the average more indicative of general unemployment in any one year, but to remove the impression that fluctuations were decreasing.   (Routh, 1959, pp. 303–4)

The Board of Trade presented the series to indicate trends, not the absolute level of unemployment in any one year. There was, in fact, a wide dispersion between different industries so that the proportions of different industries reporting could make a considerable difference to the average. In 1894, for instance, the Board of Trade showed an unweighted average for unemployment of 6.9 per cent.

67 unions with 368 000 members reported.
Of which:
16 unions with 79 000 members had less than 3 per cent unemployed
14 with 83 000 members had 10 per cent or more unemployed.
(Routh, 1959, p. 304).

I have mentioned the absence from the industries represented of agriculture, coal mining and railways: all industries of low unemployment, whose absence would thus exaggerate the levels of unemployment shown in the Board of Trade series. But this would have been greatly outweighed by the exclusion of semi-skilled and unskilled workers who were not admitted to membership of the craft unions and who, as we saw in Chapter 1, are subject to exceptionally high rates of unemployment. With these qualifications in mind, let us look at Figure 2.2, where the movements of Beveridge's index of economic activity, 1871 to 1913, are compared with the trade union unemployment returns. For unemployment I have followed Beveridge

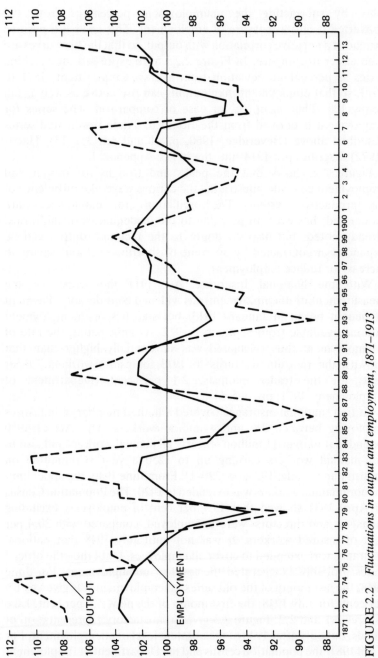

FIGURE 2.2 Fluctuations in output and employment, 1871–1913
SOURCES   see text.

who, by subtracting the unemployment percentage from 100 converted it into a measure of employment. This gives it a positive instead of a negative correlation with output, so that the two curves are then easier to compare. In Figure 2.2 I have expressed the resulting series as percentage deviation from average employment, 1871 to 1913, so that employment, like output, can rise above as well as fall below 100. This, again, is for ease of comparison. The series for employment is derived from the Board of Trade reweighted series described above (Beveridge, 1960, p. 41 and pp. 312–13). Harris (1972) describes pre-1914 statistics in her Appendix B.

Figure 2.2 shows that the peaks and troughs for output and employment coincide, illustrating the curious wave-like turbulence of the productive system. The oscillations for employment are moderated, however, in part due to the inadequacies of the series, already noted, but also no doubt to the fact that output can be expanded or contracted by overtime or shorttime without having to increase or reduce employment.

With the National Insurance Act 1911 the scope for the measurement of unemployment was widened considerably. Payment of benefit began in January 1913, but statistics of unemployment became available from September 1912. As anticipated, the rate of unemployment thus calculated was substantially higher than that shown in the trade union returns: for 1913, for insured workers, 3.6 per cent; for the trade unionists, 2.1 per cent (Department of Employment, 1971, pp. 305–6).

At first, national insurance covered a limited number of industries employing between 3¾ and 4 million workers. The Act of 1920 extended it to over 11 million – nearly all manual workers and also to non-manual workers earning up to £250 a year (Committee on Industry and Trade, 1926, pp. 220–1). From June 1940, the upper limit for non-manual workers was extended to £420. The Population Census of April 1931 showed that 15.7 per cent of employees, excluding managers and directors, were unemployed, compared with 20.4 per cent of insured workers. It was not until July 1948 that national insurance was extended to cover all employees. Until then the official series probably exaggerated the level of unemployment. For June 1948, the last month of the old series, unemployment was given as 1.9 per cent; for July 1948, the first month of the new, 1.4 per cent. Like Figures 2.1 and 2.2, Figure 2.3 gives a satisfactory representation of trends, but only after 1948 of the absolute level of unemployment. For April 1981, the population census and the Department of Employment

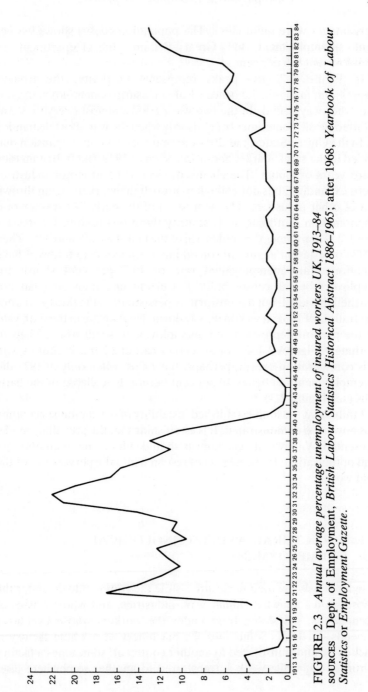

FIGURE 2.3 *Annual average percentage unemployment of insured workers UK, 1913–84*
SOURCES Dept. of Employment, *British Labour Statistics Historical Abstract 1886–1965*; after 1968, *Yearbook of Labour Statistics* or *Employment Gazette*.

percentages were quite close. The population census shows 9.8 per cent unemployment for Great Britain, the Department of Employment 9.6 per cent.

In Figure 2.2, the peaks represent prosperity, the troughs depression; in Figure 2.3, since we are measuring unemployment, it is the other way round. In the two war periods, almost everybody was allotted a task, sometimes compulsorily when the war effort demanded it. In the United States, the '20s were years of economic expansion that ended in the stock market boom and crash of 1929, but in Britain they were years of gloom. The chemical, electrical and motor industries were expanding, but not enough to absorb the workers being thrown out of other industries. The depression of the early '30s was a world phenomenon, outdoing in its severity those recorded in Figures 1.1 and 1.2. Then comes the golden age of the late '40s, '50s and '60s. Then 1977 comes as an augury of something much worse to follow. I have mentioned an unemployment rate of 15.7 per cent shown for employees by the census of 1931. Current unemployment has not reached this level, but it is obstinately persisting. In the third year after the trauma of 1931, it was on its way down. Now we are in the sixth year of the present depression and unemployment is still rising. There is nothing in Figures 2.1, 2.2 or the earlier part of 2.3 that conforms with this configuration except, perhaps, the 1920s, when only in 1927 did unemployment fall below 10 per cent before the collapse of the early '30s (see Figure 2.3).

I think that the long-established instability of the capitalist economy has now been demonstrated. It is astonishing that the prevailing model presented by university economists should still be one of equilibrium and optimisation, to the neglect of research into the perversities of the real world.

2.3   STRUCTURAL AND TECHNOLOGICAL UNEMPLOYMENT

The landlords, by their enclosures, stole the common from under the goose; in a somewhat similar way, industries, and whole classes of occupations, get stolen from under the workers whose livelihood depends on them. Sometimes the machinery of a whole factory is packed up and transported to another continent; sometimes a factory is run down, while work is transferred to another somewhere else;

sometimes industrialists invest in the same industry in a different country and compete their home factories out of existence; sometimes foreign manufacturers buy machinery from concerns who specialise in making it and whose business it is to sell to whoever will buy; sometimes it seems that the home manufacturers are overcome first by complacency, then inertia, and look on helpless while their customers abandon them. So British industries like textiles, shipbuilding and steel that once dominated world markets languish, or like motorbikes, disappear without trace.

Structural and technological unemployment are similar in effect: in the one case industries or sections of industries vanish, in the other occupations become obsolete and, in either case, workers with arduously acquired skills, are left abandoned. Of course, for this to happen there must have been a previous phase of 'structural employment' when a new industry was established and workers recruited and trained.

At the beginning of the industrial age, the machine industry of Britain destroyed the hand industries of other countries. Sir Henry Cotton witnessed this process in India and afterwards wrote, 'In 1787 the exports of Dacca muslin to England amounted to 30 lakhs (three millions) of rupees; in 1817 they had ceased altogether. The arts of spinning and weaving, which for ages afforded employment to a numerous and industrial population, have now become extinct' (Dutt, 1947, p. 102).

In Britain, at the same time, technological unemployment was afflicting the handloom weavers, though it was not until 1834 that the number of factory workers in the cotton industry overtook those working by hand. Duncan Bythell records the handloom weavers' violent reaction towards the encroachments of machines. The first factory in Manchester to operate Cartwright's power loom was attacked and burnt down in 1792, an event said to have delayed the development of power looms for many years. There were other outbreaks, culminating in the riots of 1826. 'The vandalism of 1826 was on a much grander scale than any of these previous attacks. The years 1821–5 had seen the first large-scale adoption of the power loom in cotton, whilst 1826 had brought the most severe peacetime depression the industry had yet known. Not unnaturally, the handloom weavers saw the second factor as the direct consequence of the first, and their Luddism of 1826 was a blind display of hatred against an improved machine which must be destroyed before it took away the old weavers' livelihood' (Bythell, 1969, pp. 198–204).

Between 1834 and 1844, the number of handloom weavers fell from 200 000 to 72 000. In 1854 there were 30 000, in 1862, 3000. During all this time, the industry was expanding rapidly. In 1834, cotton piece goods exported amounted to 556 million yards; in 1861 (at the commencement of the civil war in the United States) 2563 million. The industry reached the height of its glory in 1913, with the export of 7075 million yards (Mitchell and Deane, 1962, pp. 187 and 182).

What happened to the displaced handloom weavers? Some found jobs in the textile mills, though the employers preferred to employ women and girls, but they showed great prejudice against factory work and, in the outlying districts little was available. Bythell seeks for evidence, but where they disappeared to, and by what process, remains obscure (Bythell, 1969, chapter 11).

It is a calamity to be robbed of one's livelihood and there have been various episodes where the victims reacted violently in their endeavours to prevent it. In the early years of the 19th century it was done in the name of 'King Ludd' (Cole and Filson, 1951, chapter V) or, by farm workers, 'Captain Swing' (Hobsbawm and Rudé, 1969). In our own age, French farmers and truck drivers employ disruption to protect what they regard as rightfully theirs; in Britain typographers violently oppose innovations that would rob them of their status, and coalminers react violently to plans for the closure of pits.

But change in the composition of industry is constantly taking place. In 1811, the population census showed that, out of 2½ million families in the total population, 35 per cent were engaged in agriculture. In 1841, when the gainfully occupied population numbered 6.6 million, 23 per cent were in agriculture (Mitchell and Deane, 1962, p. 60). Between 1841 and 1981, the gainfully occupied population rose to nearly 25 million, while those engaged in agriculture fell from 1½ million to 644 000, that is 2.6 per cent of the labour force. Agricultural production, however, remained fairly constant, for productivity was rising fast enough to compensate for the decline in the workforce.

A decline in the number of farm workers set in about the middle of the 19th century, but in the main it seems to have been a voluntary migration from the land to the factories in pursuit of a freer and better-paid even if less secure life. Women, by contrast, continued to flock into that other field of traditional employment: domestic service. The census of 1911 counted nearly 1½ million indoor private domestic servants, of whom nearly 97 per cent were female. By 1921, the number had fallen by a third and, though it rose in the bad years of the depression, in 1951 numbers were down to 352 000, in 1971 to 198 000.

In 1911, nearly 26 per cent of economically active women were domestic servants; in 1971, just over 2 per cent.

Between 1911 and 1983, the number of women in employment almost doubled while the number of men increased by less than 20 per cent, but the scope of occupations open to women has greatly expanded. Women who might have been domestic servants seventy years ago are now nurses, teachers, secretaries, shop assistants, or in other jobs that enable them to live their private lives safe from the gaze of their employers.

In Table 1.3 we saw the changes in industrial employment that took place between 1979 and 1984, when cylical employment was the dominant influence. Table 2.1, by contrast, emphasises long-term structural changes by comparing 1911 with 1971, both years of low unemployment.

The gainfully occupied population of Great Britain increased by 32.3 per cent between 1911 and 1971, so the workforce in any industrial group would have had to increase by the same percentage just to hold its own. Agriculture, mining, textiles, leather and clothing have

TABLE 2.1 *Employment in industries or industrial groups, Great Britain 1911 and 1971*

| | Nos. in thousands | | |
	1911	1971	1971 as % of 1911
Agriculture, forestry, fishing	1499	635	42
Mining and quarrying	1128	391	35
Ceramics, glass, chemicals	348	824	237
Metal manufacture	509	551	108
Engineering, shipbuilding, metal goods	1490	3620	243
Textiles, leather, clothing	2611	1114	43
Other manufactures	1260	1977	157
Building, civil engineering	950	1669	176
Gas, electricity, water	116	362	312
Transport and communication	1416	1564	110
Distributive trades	2133	3016	141
Finance	199	952	478
Public administration and defence	701	1572	224
Professional services	789	2901	368
Miscellaneous services	2783	2357	85
	17941	23733*	132

*including 177 000 inadequately described or working outside the UK.
SOURCE Routh, 1980, p. 42.

conspicuously failed to do so. In 1911, of every hundred workers, 29 were employed in one or other of these groups; in 1971, only 9.

The proportion engaged in the distributive trades has not changed much: 11.9 per cent in 1911 and 12.7 per cent in 1971. The leading growth industries have been:

	Per cent of workforce	
	1911	1971
Engineering, etc.	8.3	15.4
Gas, electricity, water	0.6	1.5
Finance	1.1	4.0
Public administration and defence	3.9	6.6
Professional services	4.4	12.2
	18.3	39.7

There has been a considerable transfer of workers in these sixty years, on the one hand to metal-using industries, and on the other to white-collar industries. Have those industries where employment has declined left a residue of unemployment? And are there relatively few unemployed attached to industries that have expanded? Table 2.2 provides a test. In June 1971, there were 664 000 unemployed workers who had last worked in the groups of industries shown. Column 1 shows the percentage that each industry contributed to the total. Table 2.1 shows that there was a total of 23 556 000 workers employed in these industries in 1971. Column 2 of Table 2.2 shows the percentage that each industry contributed to this total. Column 3 shows column 1 as a percentage of column 2. An industry that had the same proportion of the unemployed as of the employed would score 100 in column 3.

Agriculture, forestry and fishing had fewer unemployed than would have been expected on this basis and scored only 85, despite the great fall in employment shown in Table 2.1. Mining and quarrying had a high score for unemployment, that accords with its performance in Table 2.1, but the textile group has much lower unemployment than might have been expected, considering the magnitude of its decline.

The groups that had expanded (Table 2.1) all had low scores in column 3, especially professional services, but building and civil engineering, that showed considerable expansion in Table 2.1, had a far higher rate of unemployment than any other group.

These observations suggest further hypotheses for testing: that unemployment in ceramics, glass, chemicals etc. has been technological rather than structural; that in construction the cause has

TABLE 2.2 *Employment and unemployment in industries or industrial groups, Great Britain, June 1971*

| Industry | percentage distribution | | |
	(1) % of unemployed	(2) % of employed	(3) (1) as % of (2)
Agriculture, forestry and fishing	2.3	2.7	85
Mining and quarrying	3.2	1.6	200
Ceramics, glass, chemicals	3.5	2.1	166
Metal manufacture	4.4	2.3	191
Engineering, shipbuilding, etc.	19.3	15.4	125
Textiles, leather, clothing	5.2	4.7	111
Other manufacturing	9.1	8.4	108
Building, civil engineering	17.7	7.0	253
Gas, electricity, water	1.3	1.5	87
Transport and communication	6.1	6.6	92
Distributive trades	10.0	12.7	79
Finance	2.3	4.0	57
Public administration and defence	4.4	6.6	35
Professional services	2.8	12.2	23
Miscellaneous services	8.3	9.9	84
	100	100	

SOURCES unemployment, *Annual Abstract of Statistics*, pp. 138–41; employment, as Table 2.1.

been one of the cyclical down-turns to which that industry is peculiarly prone; that in metal manufacture the cause of high unemployment has been structural; that in agriculture, forestry and fishing, a voluntary exodus has reduced the residue of unemployed. In Section 2.4 of this chapter I shall try to distinguish in the data between structural, technological and cyclical unemployment.

Since 1971, cyclical unemployment has swamped structural unemployment, but sometimes the two have combined to induce the industrial changes shown in Table 1.3. If structural decline takes place slowly enough, then changes in employment can take place by natural wastage. Workers who retire or who leave for jobs in other industries are not replaced. This occurs at times of full employment. But at other times, structural decline may combine with technological and cyclical changes to destroy jobs faster than they can be replaced. If an employer dismisses someone because his or her job has been eliminated, the employee is declared redundant and receives compensation in terms of the Employment Protection Act of 1975.

In the first quarter of 1984, 122 416 employees received statutory redundancy pay amounting to £188.8 million. A bit more than half was paid by the employers concerned, the balance coming from the Redundancy Fund which is financed by contributions from employers and employees. The highest number of redundancies came from the distributive trades (12 000), followed by construction (11 900) and mechanical engineering (11 100) (*Employment Gazette*, July 1984, p. 330). Redundancy figures are a key indicator of the state of economic health.

In 1979, there were 187 000 notified redundancies (only those of ten or more employees have to be notified). In 1980, the number was 494 000. In 1981, there were more than half-a-million, but they are now diminishing, with 108 000 in the first half of 1984 (*Employment Gazette*, July 1984, p. S40). It does not follow, of course, that the redundant worker may not get another job in the same occupation somewhere else – merely that the employer is ceasing to offer the job in his employ.

Employers are constantly trying to economise in labour and other costs of production by improving their technology. Where there are big changes affecting large numbers of workers, employers often enter into a 'no redundancies' agreement and proceed to retrain their workers or otherwise adapt them to the new jobs. The Work Research Unit of the Department of Employment was established in 1974 to advise on and monitor the introduction of new technology, particularly that concerned with office work and administration where change has been particularly fast. Richard Smith, in a report published by the Unit in 1981, summarised the possibilities:

> Longer-term, more sophisticated communications systems may even remove the need for offices as we know them. Electronic person-to-person linking systems, group teleconferencing, data and text transmission, and electronic filing systems theoretically allow people to work independently of any geographical location and conduct their business activities from their own private work-station located in the home, the hotel, or even a car. Already such systems exist and there is no doubt that their use will increase, particularly for 'mobile' people such as salesmen, who can now communicate orders direct into the company's computer system – thereby removing the need for clerical jobs in the head office. For most office workers, however, a more likely move is towards using the new system to give greater efficiency within the existing office complex. (Work Research Unit, 1981, p. 3)

The new systems will cause the reversal of a trend that has been asserting itself since the turn of the century. In the 1890s, the men copyists, with their beautiful copperplate script, began to be eliminated by the 'female typewriters' who were regarded as peculiarly fitted to operate the new writing machines. Fortunately for the copyists there were other office jobs to which they could turn, so that the number of male clerical workers rose from 654 000 in 1911 to 959 000 in 1971. But during the Second World War, the men lost their numerical superiority. In 1911, the women numbered 179 000; in 1971 their numbers had risen to 2 453 000 (Routh, 1980, p. 24).

From 1911 to 1931, the number of women clerical workers tripled; from 1931 to 1951, it doubled; from 1951 to 1971, it rose by three-quarters. By 1971, of all women employed 27 per cent were office workers, more than the combined numbers of shop assistants, nurses and teachers. But the rate of increase was losing its momentum, and sometime between 1981 and 1983, it went into reverse.

The population census of 1981 lists 2 736 020 women clerical workers: an increase over 1971 of 11.5 per cent, only ⅓ of the rate in operation between 1951 and 1971. By 1983, their numbers were in decline. Clerical and related workers is employment amounted to:

	Male	Female
	(thousands)	
1981	988	2877
1983	920	2758

Clerical and related as a percentage of all workers in employment were:

	Male	*Female*
1981	7.2	31.4
1983	6.8	29.3

(For 1981: Census 1981 Economic Activity Great Britain, pp. 106–7. 1983: *Employment Gazette*, July 1984, p. 325. 'Clerical and related' include clerical supervisors, telephonists, postmen and mail sorters.)

There is another bit of evidence to support this view: the Department of Employment publishes each year statistics showing the proportions of white-collar and blue-collar workers in manufacturing industry. Amongst the male employees in 1948, 15.2 per cent were white-collar, amongst the females, 17.9 per cent. Year after year the proportions increased, until:

Percentage of white-collar employees

	Males	Females	All
September 1981	28.7	31.8	29.6
September 1982	29.5	33.3	30.6
September 1983	28.9	28.7	28.8

(*British Labour Statistics Historical Abstract*, p. 276. *Employment Gazette*, March 1982, p. S19; November 1981, p. S14; January 1984, p. S18.)

In the past seventy or eighty years there has been a substantial increase in the employment of women as teachers, nurses, office workers and shop assistants. Now teaching and nursing languish for lack of funds, retailing has reached a plateau and office work is set for a decline.

Computers are removing much of the tedium from office work, and robots are taking over the drudgery of the assembly line, of whose ill-effects Adam Smith warned two hundred years ago:

> The man whose whole life is spent in performing a few simple operations . . . has no occasion to exert his understanding . . . He naturally loses, therefore, the habit of such exertion, and generally becomes as stupid and ignorant as it is possible for a human creature to become. The torpor of his mind renders him, not only incapable of relishing or bearing a part in any rational conversation, but of conceiving any generous, noble, or tender sentiment, and consequently of forming any just judgment concerning many even of the ordinary duties of private life.   (Smith, 1776, p. 782)

We need not regret the disappearance of office routine or the endless repetition of the assembly line, but other changes in technology leave a sense of loss, for instance amongst printing craftsmen who go over to computerised techniques. The Work Research Unit reports in one case study:

> Having done so, and having settled into the new system, as a matter of work routine, most now feel a sense of deprivation through the loss of their traditional craft skills. There is, too, a sense of a loss of pride in the work itself, since there is general recognition that many of the tasks involved in the new technology could be carried out by people with fairly low levels of training and without necessarily having a print-industry background. This is particularly true of the keyboard operators, who fully recognize that any competent typist could quickly learn to operate their typesetting equipment.   (Richard Smith and Terry Quinlan, 1982, p. 16)

The trade unions have been understandably concerned with the impact of the new technology on jobs and the quality of working life. Agreements with employers cover a guarantee of existing jobs, provisions for voluntary redundancy and for retraining (TUC, 1980; Association of Professional, Executive and Computer Staff, 1979 and 1980). The Electronics Economic Development Committee and the Information Technology Economic Development Committee have published a report on the impact on jobs of advanced information systems, illustrated by case studies (National Economic Development Office, 1984). The European Social Fund provides funds for the modernisation of small and medium firms and for the retraining of workers overtaken by new technologies (Commission of the European Communities, 1984).

2.4 STRUCTURAL, TECHNOLOGICAL OR CYCLICAL UNEMPLOYMENT?

Let us begin by examining the quarter-century after the second World War when what looks, in retrospect, like the British miracle took place. It is true that the country was being overtaken and even surpassed by other industrial countries, which occasioned that deep gloom that Britons like to feel when they are enjoying themselves. It was, in fact, a time of solid achievement. Between 1948 and 1973, the output of production industries (mining, manufacturing, construction, gas, electricity and water) increased by 115 per cent, while numbers employed hardly changed. Output per worker had more than doubled. (It is not possible to measure the output of 'non-production' or service industries, because they do not have a material product. In national accounting, the output of the civil service, military, police, health, education, entertainment and distributive services is deemed to be measured by the incomes of those concerned.)

While real income and expenditure rose, people were enjoying a sense of security unprecedented in the modern age. For much of the 1950s, employment exchanges had more vacant jobs on their registers than there were unemployed workers. There was, as we have noted, an excess of workers without skills or qualifications, but the education level of young people was gradually rising, and the labour force was able to absorb increasing numbers of women. Between 1951 and 1971, the numbers in professional occupations rose from 1.5 million to nearly 2.8 million. In economic forecasts, the term 'depression' went out of use in favour of the milder term 'recession' and even these, in the United Kingdom, were brief and slight.

Thus the unemployment that we are able to identify in Table 2.3 is likely to have been structural or technological rather than cyclical. Look first at the two columns relating to the years 1948–58. Structural unemployment is occasioned by a permanent decline in output, but there are only two industrial orders where that is in evidence: shipbuilding and marine engineering (output −7 per cent), and leather, leather goods and fur (output −28 per cent). Employment

TABLE 2.3   *Changes in output and employment, production industries
United Kingdom*

	1948–58		1958–68		1968–73	
	O	E	O	E	O	E
Index of production industries	134	111	142	96	113	93
Mining and quarrying	104	98	81	57	83	75
Drink and tobacco	110	106	147	94	123	81
Food	136	130	126	99	109	93
Coke ovens, oil refineries, etc.	244	143	156	61	131	70
General chemical and allied products	161	120	196	100	134	96
Metal manufacture	122	107	125	102	102	89
Mechanical engineering	142	119	153	110	111	91
Electrical engineering	161	139	184	126	133	98
Shipbuilding and marine engineering	93	91	67	65	95	96
Vehicles and aircraft	193	129	140	66	105	98
Metal goods n.e.s.	114	101	123	112	105	97
Textiles	102	94	131	79	112	86
Leather, leather goods and fur	82	81	92	88	97	87
Clothing and footwear	115	101	124	81	113	93
Bricks, cement	126	100	171	91	116	77
Pottery	100	91	131	98 }	131	59
Glass	133	113	167	106 }		
Timber, furniture	133	99	133	114	125	99
Paper, printing and publishing	169	124	151	110	117	107
Other manufacturing	151	118	170	124	122	107
Construction	121	103	147	113	103	91
Gas, electricity and water	169	117	171	110	129	82

O = output;   E = employment.

SOURCES   Index of Industrial Production – *Annual Abstracts of Statistics*; Employment – *British Labour Statistics Year Books*.

fell at almost equal pace, so that there is no sign of technological unemployment. The only other falls of employment of any importance were in textiles (−6 per cent) and pottery (−9 per cent). Here, output did not fall, so that the decline in employment may be attributed to improved technology.

Now examine the period 1958–68. The output of mining and quarrying registers a substantial decline, and so does shipbuilding. Leather output falls some more, but not so much as in the previous period. But in mining, employment is down much more than output, signifying a dramatic increase in output per man. Thus the fall in employment was part structural, as coal was ousted by oil, and part technological as facework was mechanised.

Eleven of the orders were free of unemployment and, of these, eight increased employment by 10 per cent or more. There were big increases in output per worker, but most industries were able to increase their sales more than proportionately. Technological unemployment appeared, however in:

	1968 as % of 1958		Job loss
	Employment	Output	000s
Coke ovens, oil refineries etc.	61	156	37
Vehicles and aircraft	66	140	403.5
Textiles	79	131	185
Clothing and footwear	81	124	110
Bricks, cement	91	171	8

In 1968–73, the decline in output continued in mining, shipbuilding and leather. Output continued to rise in other industries, substantially in some cases, but (except in paper, printing and publishing, and other manufacturing) not enough to offset the employment effect of the rise in output per worker. The overall loss of employment was 7 per cent, or 771 000.

The end of this golden age came in 1973, with a strong rise in commodity (raw materials) prices, followed by the OPEC-administered rise in the price of oil. The rise in output that had characterised the preceding 25 years disappeared. The United Kingdom was protected by the arrival of North Sea oil and gas. With them, total output was up 3 per cent in 1979 compared with 1973; without them, down 4 per cent.

In the ten years to 1958, the output of production industries rose 34 per cent, and to 1968 another 42 per cent. In the five years, 1968 to 1973, the rise was 13 per cent, nearly 2.5 per cent per year. If the same quite modest rate had been maintained from 1973 to 1979, the increase in output would have been almost 16 per cent instead of the 3 per cent that we have noted. The output of bricks and cement, and telegraph and telephone equipment fell 29 per cent, other industries 10 or 15 per cent. But increases were recorded for:

	1979 as % of 1973
Drink and tobacco	113
Food	101
Chemicals and allied	113
of which pharmaceuticals	132
Electrical engineering	112
of which electronic computers	317
Instrument engineering	119
Clothing and footwear	105
China and earthenware	120
Glass	102
Furniture and upholstery	105
General printing and publishing	106
Other manufacturing industry	107
Gas, electricity, water	118

The number of employees in production industries fell by 680 000 (7 per cent). The reduction extended to all industries except chemicals, and gas, electricity and water.

Over the next four years, the reduction in employment was drastic. Two million jobs were lost, 22.4 per cent of all jobs. The only sections to increase employment were electronic computers (+19 per cent) and radio, radar and electronic capital goods (+11 per cent).

While employment fell by 22 per cent, output (including oil and natural gas) fell by 6 per cent, so that productivity (output per worker) rose by 21 per cent. Now we are in real difficulty in our attempt to distinguish cyclical from structural from technological unemployment. Without the changes in technique that enabled 94 per cent of output to be attained by 78 per cent of the workforce, the fall in sales would have been more severe. Industrial companies were fighting for their lives against competition, national and international, intensified by world-wide depression. In this setting, technological and organisational improvements are likely to have reduced rather than increased the loss of jobs.

Nor is it possible to identify structural unemployment: reductions in sales from which firms and industries will not recover, even with the return to general prosperity. Textiles, clothing and pottery have, in the past twenty years, shown great enterprise in improving their international competitiveness by advances in quality and design. One cannot say, *a priori*, that traditional industries are doomed to decline. At this point, the statistics peter out as sources of information and one has to find out from the decision-makers themselves the likely prospects for their firms and industries.

3 Theory: Petty to Keynes

3.1 LINES OF DESCENT

Why study theories of unemployment, you may ask, when none of them has produced a formula to end it? Or, if it has, it is a cure unacceptable to governments and electorates, or perhaps neutralised by counter-cures propounded by other theorists. But despite the fact that there is none that we can point to and say, 'This is demonstrably true', the theories must still be studied. From them we derive the vocabulary and systems of classification that are necessary preliminaries to thinking about the subject. To a critical mind they offer warnings, too, of the fallibility of the human mind and its susceptibility to theoretic blight (Walker, 1943) in its enthusiasm to escape, as Adam Smith put it, the jarring and discordant appearances of unexplained phenomena. Since the theories conflict, they challenge our critical faculties to distinguish between truth and error, and so construct a higher synthesis. I devote this chapter to propounding the basic theories, the next to presenting their modern counterparts, and Chapter 5 to bringing them to judgment.

We may distinguish two lines of descent, the one leading to the Welfare State, where a rising proportion of resources go into public consumption, and where human behaviour is understood as a product of social and psychological forces; the other to the market economy, whose motive-power is attributed to private consumption, self-interest and pecuniary gain. On the one side, Macmillan and Heath Conservatives and the Labour Party; on the other, Thatcher and Reagan Conservatives drawing inspiration from monetarism, supply-side economics and rational expectations. Each side can invoke the aid of philosophers, political scientists and sociologists and, over the years, each has had the support of powerful teams of economists whose lines of descent are roughly as follows:

Common ancestors
Sir William Petty (1623–87)
Adam Smith (1723–90)
Thomas Robert Malthus (1766–1834)
John Stuart Mill (1806–73)

Welfare State	*Market economy*
Pierre le Pesant, Sieur de Boisguillebert (1646–1714)	John Locke (1632–1704)
Simonde de Sismondi (1773–1842)	Sir Dudley North (1641–91)
	Richard Cantillon (1697–1743)
	Jean Baptiste Say (1767–1832)
Thomas Edward Cliffe Leslie (1827–82)	David Ricardo (1772–1823)
	Harriet Martineau (1802–76)
Arnold Toynbee (1852–83)	Leon Walras (1834–1910)
John Atkinson Hobson (1858–1940)	Alfred Marshall (1842–1924)
	John Bates Clark (1847–1938)
Wesley Clair Mitchell (1874–1948)	
William Henry Beveridge (1879–1963)	
John Maynard Keynes (1883–1946)	

You may think it strange that those I list as 'common ancestors' should span two centuries, but the four people there listed each embrace and contribute to both streams. The two sides remain in conflict, yet each draws inspiration from and appeals to the authority of each of the four. It is not unusual for a great thinker to harbour contradictory ideas and to lend his authority to both, a process to which Smith and Mill were particularly prone.

3.2   A SELF-REGULATING SYSTEM

The common ancestors and the market economists argue that the economy regulates itself automaticaly, to the benefit of all, or that it would do so if it could be freed from government control. These arguments were no doubt popular amongst the merchants and bankers of the 17th and 18th centuries, as they are to the merchants and bankers of today. Today governments on occasion donate large sums of money to keep their bankers and manufacturers out of trouble, but in the 17th and 18th centuries it was the businessmen who were expected to pay, their efforts at accumulation thus seriously impeded by the extravagant despots of those times. Petty publicised the slogan '*vadere sicut vult*', which is Latin for '*laissez-faire*', and Locke and North elaborated the mechanism through which this would operate to the good of all. 'All things that are bought and sold raise and fall their price, in proportion as there are more buyers or sellers' (Locke, 1692, p. 39).

The reciprocal rights and obligations of earlier societies had been replaced by the cash nexus; human relations were transformed into pecuniary relations. It was in their capacity as buyers and sellers that people exercised their freedom of choice, thus guiding resources into those lines in which their usefulness was maximised. Richard Cantillon, an Irishman operating in Paris, drew on his experience as banker and financier, to explain how the system worked. 'Suppose the Butchers on one side and the Buyers on the other. The price of Meat will be settled after some altercations, and a pound of Beef will be in value to a piece of silver pretty nearly as the whole Beef offered for sale in the Market is to all the silver brought there to buy Beef. This proportion is come at by bargaining.' This was the principle of 'perfect competition' that would in due course be presented as the model of capitalism (Higgs, 1959, pp. 117–19).

Cantillon's book formed the basis of the doctrines of that coterie of economists in France who became known as 'Physiocrats'. François Quesnay, their leader, proclaimed, 'The whole magic of a well-ordered society is that each man works for others, while believing that he is working for himself. This magic, the general character and effects of which are revealed by the subject we are studying, shows us that the Supreme Being bestowed upon us as father the principles of economic harmony, when he condescended to announce and prescribe them to us, as God, in the form of religious laws' (Routh, 1975, p. 75). The principles of economics, you will note, were not invented by man but, like the Ten Commandments, prescribed by God.

The principles were inexorable. A tradesman who tried to sell at prices higher than those offered elsewhere would be 'eaten up by expenses' and ruined. As with commodities, so with workers: their supply to different occupations 'is naturally proportioned to the demand for them' (Higgs, 1959, pp. 51 and 23). The operation of the laws is shown nowhere so forcefully as in the supply of and demand for people: 'Men multiply like Mice in a barn if they have unlimited Means of Subsistence': 'a single generation suffices to push the increase of

Population as far as the produce of the Land will supply means of subsistence' (Higgs, 1959, p. 81).

Adam Smith echoed Cantillon in the *Wealth of Nations*: 'Every species of animals naturally multiplies in proportion to the means of their subsistence, and no species can ever multiply beyond it. But in civilized society it is only among the inferior ranks of people that the scantiness of subsistence can set limits to the further multiplication of the human species; and it can do so in no other way than by destroying a great part of the children which their fruitful marriages produce'. Why then did the 'superior ranks' not multiply exponentially? Because of the delicacy of their women folk. A half-starved Highland woman often had twenty children, but 'a pampered fine lady is often incapable of bearing any, and is generally exhausted by two or three' (Smith, 1776, pp. 96–7).

Adam Smith contradicts his own gloomy views by describing how the money wages of labour had risen in the 18th century while prices fell, so that real wages had greatly advanced (Smith, 1776, pp. 94–5). Malthus, by contrast, in his first essay on population, admitted of no appeasement in the war waged by nature against man. Population was capable of doubling every twenty-five years; it was inconceivable that food production could do more than increase by equal increments. The consequence? 'sickly seasons, epidemics, pestilence, and plague, advance in terrific array. . . Should success be still incomplete, gigantic inevitable famine stalks in the rear and with one mighty blow, levels the population with the food of the world' (Routh, 1975, pp. 109–10). It was this description that led Thomas Carlyle to refer to economics as 'the dismal science'.

While economics was and remains a predominantly masculine preserve, it was two women who popularised it and thereby nurtured some of the great economists of the 19th century. Mrs Jane Haldimand Marcet (1769–1858) in her fascinating dialogues, *Conversations on Political Economy* and *Rich and Poor*, summarised economic thought on, *inter alia*, the problem of poverty: 'giving encourages beggars, and yet they are not better off. If you double the quantity of halfpence, you double the number of beggars' and 'It is the will of God,' answered John, 'that children should die if their parents do not provide for them so that they may live' (Marcet, 1851, p. 4, and 1939, p. 76).

Harriet Martineau (1802–76) presented her ideas in monthly stories, under the title of *Illustrations of Political Economy*. Falls in price, to which various trades were subject, must be accompanied by falls in wages, and this is what happened in the firm of Bernard & Wallace.

'The first reduction was taken quietly; the second excited murmurs among the ignorant, and fear and sorrow among the clear-sighted . . .; the third occasioned threats of actual rebellion. Some of the men refused to work for such wages'. In the resulting redundancies, the least industrious and able were dismissed, in the hopes that they would carry their labour where it was more wanted (Martineau, 1832, vol. II, pp. 90–1).

The moral was clear: if demand falls, then prices must fall and workers must take their share. It was an unfounded prejudice that the interest of the two sides could be opposed.

What could be done to lessen the number of the indigent? It was a matter of supply and demand: the limitation of population would *ipso facto* raise the share of each worker in the wages fund (the stock of resources, owned by employers, destined for the support of labour, and deemed to be invariable between harvests). Adam Smith had clearly stated, 'The demand for those who live by wages, it is evident, cannot increase but in proportion to the increase of the funds which are destined for the payment of wages' (Smith, 1776, p. 86).

It was the will of God, as Mrs Marcet had explained, and any attempt to subvert the divine will would lead to further disaster. In Miss Martineau's Tale No. VIII, 'Cousin Marshall', Mr Burke, the young surgeon, explains the problem to his sister Louisa, 'There is harm enough done by the poor taking for granted that they are to be supplied with medicine and advice gratis all their lives: the evil is increasing every day by their looking on assistance in child-birth as their due; and if they learn to expect food and warmth in like manner, their misery will be complete' (p. 38).

These were the prevailing views of what we now call unemployment. Very soon, Malthus's view of population, derived from Cantillon through Smith, would be abandoned, but the conception of a mechanical economy, governed by 'iron laws', has survived to the present day. It was Nassau William Senior (1790–1864) who, in his letters to Malthus and his Oxford lectures as Drummond Professor of Political Economy, refuted the theory of population. He did it in the simplest possible way. Malthus had asserted a tendency for population to outrun subsistence. Look back over history, Senior argued, and you will observe that the reverse applies. The famines of earlier days are unheard of, though population had trebled or quadrupled (Senior, 1966, p. 48).

This did not have the effect of softening Senior's feelings towards the poor. Beveridge's Index of Industrial Activity (Table 2.1, above) shows a sharp drop after 1825, reaching a trough in 1832. Senior viewed these hard times not as the downturn of a trade cycle but as themselves the result of the Poor Law, with its 'indefinite multiplication of an idle, improvident and vicious population' (Levy, 1970, p. 250). His first 'elementary proposition of the science of political economy' was 'That every man desires to obtain additional Wealth with as little sacrifice as possible' (Senior, 1836, p. v), and from this it followed that if you paid people for being idle, they would be more idle than ever. So it was that the Royal Commission on the Poor Laws, 1832–4, of which Senior was a moving spirit, recommended that outdoor relief should be abolished – that is, relief that permitted a man to live at home. Pauperism amongst able-bodied people was rarely due to 'blameless want', but to indolence, improvidence or vice. Relief should be given only in a well-regulated workhouse. 'The dissolute poor hate its cleanliness, its regularity, its confinement, its classification, its labour, and its absence of stimulants' (Levy, 1970, p. 251).

3.2.2 Say's Law

The years 1805 to 1823 were marked by severe industrial fluctuations (see Table 2.1 above) in the course of which occurred one of the most celebrated controversies in the annals of economic thought: on the one side, Ricardo and Say; on the other, Malthus and Sismondi. Keynes wrote, in retrospect, 'the almost total obliteration of Malthus's line of approach and the complete domination of Ricardo's for a period of a hundred years has been a disaster to the progress of economics' (Keynes, 1933, p. 117).

The argument was over whether there could be such a thing as a 'general glut' applicable to all commodities at the same time. It was understandable, Ricardo and Say argued, that one or two commodities might be over-supplied through the misjudgement of the suppliers, but a general glut was impossible because 'supply created its own demand'. Say explained it thus: 'It is worth while to remark, that a product is no sooner created, than it from that instant, affords a market for other products to the full extent of its own value. When the producer has put the finishing hand to his product, he is most anxious to sell it immediately, lest its value should vanish in his hands. Nor is he less anxious to dispose of the money he may get for it; for the value of the money is also perishable. But the only way of getting rid of money is in the purchase of some product or other. Thus, the mere circumstances of the creation of one product immediately opens a vent for other products' (Say, 1821, p. 167).

The same rules applied to labour. If there were an excess of it, its price would fall until the excess had disappeared. Malthus had suggested that profits had fallen because of over-saving. But if profits fell, wages would rise because, according to Ricardo's labour theory of value, the proceeds of sales were divided between wages and profits. But if profits fell, capitalists would stop saving and workers would be thrown out of work. Malthus had said, 'we know from repeated experience that the money price of labour never falls till many workmen have been for some time out of work'. But Ricardo knew no such thing: workers would very soon reduce their demands so that not many would be thrown out of work. 'All general reasoning I apprehend is in favour of my view of this question, and for why should some agree to go without any wages while others were most liberally rewarded' (Sraffa, 1962, vol. II p. 23 *et seq.*).

The argument pivoted on the virtues of parsimony. Malthus recommended 'unproductive expenditure' or extravagance to keep the economy moving, but this was repugnant to the 'general reasoning' of the orthodox view. It had been David Hume (1711–76) who had stressed the beneficial social effect of the rising opulence of private men – provided they did not squander their money. Writing in the days of merchant capitalism, he argued that the merchant's passion for profit was his special virtue. 'And this is the reason why trade encreases frugality, and why, among merchants, there is the same overplus of misers above prodigals, as, among possessors of land, there is the contrary' (Rotwein, 1955, pp. 51–4).

Adam Smith elaborated this and it became a tenet of orthodox thought. This is the key passage: 'Whatever a person saves from his revenue he adds to his capital, and either employs it himself in maintaining an additional number of productive hands, or enables some other person to do so, by lending it to him for an interest, that is, for a share of the profits. As the capital of an individual can be increased only by what he saves from his annual revenue or his annual gains, so the capital of a society, which is the same with that of all the individuals who compose it, can be increased only in the same manner'. And he clinches the argument in a fateful sentence: 'What is annually saved is as regularly consumed as what is annually spent, and nearly in the same time too; but it is consumed by a different set of people' (Smith, 1776, pp. 337–8).

3.2.3 The Marginalists: Jevons to Pigou

By the middle of the 19th century, the economists had almost completed their picture of capitalism. The 'jarring and discordant appearance of unexplained phenomena' (as Adam Smith had put it), engendering a 'tumult of the imagination', had been allayed, the imagination restored 'to that tone of tranquility and composure, which is both most agreeable to itself, and most suitable to its nature' (Campbell and Skinner, 1982, p. 84). In its place they had put Quesnay's 'magic of a well-ordered society'. Malthus's theory of population, with its unprepossessing face, had been dropped, and Mill, who had made much of the wages fund, was about to renegue on it. There remained only Ricardo's labour theory of value, that so awkwardly identified labour as the source of all wealth and which, in the hands of the socialists, according to Knut Wicksell, 'became a terrible weapon against the existing order' (Wicksell, 1901, p. 28). This was banished by three books that appeared independently in the 1870s: W. Stanley Jevons, *The Theory of Political Economy* (1871), Carl Menger, *Principles of Economics* (1871), and Leon Walras, *Elements of Pure Economics* (1874). The new theories showed that nations advanced not by revolution, nor indeed any sort of violent change, but by constantly-occurring little incremental adjustments – a little more of this, a little less of that, by which every consumer maximised pleasure and minimised pain, and every entrepreneur maximised output and minimised effort.

Forces were constantly tending to equilibrium at which these happy outcomes would be achieved. The system could be presented graphically by a series of curves: on the vertical axis cost or price was measured, on the horizontal, quantity supplied or demanded. The achievement of equilibrium depended on the prevalence of upward-sloping supply curves and downward-sloping demand curves: the more that was produced, the higher was the cost of each additional unit, while the more that was consumed the less was the satisfaction obtained from each additional unit.

It is the theory of marginal productivity that concerns us here, for it purports to explain the operation of the labour market. For more general studies, see Roll (1973), chapters VIII and IX, Heilbroner (1972) chapter VII, or Hutchison (1953), Part I.

The demand for labour was derived from the demand for goods and services. If the selling-price of an additional unit of a commodity exceeded the cost of production, producers would produce more of it.

Higher output would cause selling price to fall and cost of production to rise. Equilibrium would reign at the point where they were equal. In the case of labour, if the rise in product occasioned by an additional unit of labour sold for more than the cost of that unit, the employer would employ that additional unit of labour, and would continue to employ additional units until the addition to costs equalled the additional sales revenue. At this point, the marginal product of labour would be equal to the wage. This is the marginal productivity theory.

Thus wage, selling price, quantity sold and level of employment were all objectively decided and formed part of a determinate system. If there were excess supply of labour, competition for jobs would cause wages to fall until full employment was restored. If there were excess demand for labour, wages would be bid up until, at the wage rate so established, no jobs remained unfilled. Any unemployment that remained after this process had run its course would be strictly voluntary, showing that those concerned would rather remain unemployed than compete for available jobs. As John Bates Clark (1847–1938) explained it, 'As real as gravitation is the force that draws actual pay of men *toward* a standard that is set by the final productivity law. . . . what we are able to produce by means of labor, is determined by what a final unit of mere labor can add to the product that can be created without its aid' (Clark, 1899, p. 180).

So if workers were unemployed, it must be because they were demanding more than their labour could produce. They were unemployed because they chose to be. Supply of goods was also demand for goods; supply of labour was demand for the products of labour. Say's Law ruled, and unemployment was ruled out of the economics syllabus. Alfred Marshall made three references to unemployment, or 'inconstancy of employment' in his *Principles of Economics* the first edition of which appeared in 1890 and the last in 1920. This was the standard text for English-language economics at least until 1940. 'The doctrine on unemployment is thus easily summarised. In any occupation in which employment is irregular, pay must be proportionately higher' (Marshall, 1961, p. 555). His next reference has the marginal heading, 'The inconstancy of employment in modern industry is apt to be exaggerated' (p. 687). In the final reference he quotes Mill's exposition of Say's Law: 'All sellers are inevitably, and by the meaning of the word, buyers. Could we suddenly double the productive powers of the country, we should double the supply of commodities in every market; but we should, by the same stroke, double the purchasing power . . . everybody would be able to buy twice as much, because everyone would have twice as much to offer in exchange' (pp. 710–11).

Marshall then adds two paragraphs, quoted from his own *Economics of Industry* (written jointly with his wife and published in 1879), taken from the early writings of John Stuart Mill (though Marshall has apparently forgotten this for he makes no acknowledgement). The passage begins, 'But though men have the power to purchase they may not choose to use it'. He describes the occurrence of crisis and depression, and offers in explanation, 'The chief cause of the evil is a want of confidence. The greater part of it could be removed almost in an instant if confidence could return, touch all industries with her magic wand, and make them continue their production and their demand for the wares of others'. But the significance of this portentous passage passes him by: he allots to it one page and six lines in a book of 858 pages. Disorganisation of consumption is a contributory cause, 'But a remedy is not to be got by a study of consumption, as has been alleged by some hasty writers' (p. 172).

This view was maintained right into the depths of the depression of the 1930s. So, Professor Edwin Cannan in his presidential address to the Royal Economic Society in 1932: 'General unemployment appears when asking too much is a general phenomenon . . . [the world] should learn to submit to declines of money-income without squealing' (Routh, 1975, p. 268). And in 1933, Professor Pigou, Marshall's successor at Cambridge, 'There will always be at work a strong tendency for wage-rates to be so related to demand that everybody is employed' (Pigou, 1933, p. 252).

3.3 PRECURSORS OF THE WELFARE STATE

The market economists believed in the beneficent power of competition operating in its habitat of the free market. But if the heavy hand of government replaced the invisible hand of God or nature, hideous discord would ensue. The precursors of the Welfare State, by contrast, believed that the market system suffered from serious defects that demanded public intervention, or might even be incurable.

Thus, Sir William Petty, despite his assertion of *vadere sicut vult*, believed that the way to deal with poverty was to put the poor beggars to work. Highways could be made broad, firm and even, rivers made navigable, trees planted for timber, delight and fruit; bridges built;

mines sunk, iron manufactured. Indeed, if their work were without expense of foreign commodities, 'then 'tis no matter if it be employed to build a useless Pyramid upon *Salisbury Plain*, bring the Stones at *Stonehenge* to *Tower-Hill*, or the like; for at worst this would keep their mindes to discipline and obedience, and their bodies to a patience of more profitable labours when need should require it' (Hull, 1899, pp. 29 and 31). Keynes was to present the same proposals 250 years later.

But who should pay these men? The answer, everybody. There was a superfluity that was otherwise lost and wasted, or wantonly spent. 'Or in case there be no overplus, than 'tis fit to retrench a little from the delicacy of others feeding in quantity or quality; few men spending less than double of what might suffice them as to the bare necessities of nature'.

Petty's friend John Graunt (1620–74) took a somewhat different view: 'the vast number of *Beggars* swarming up and down this City, do all live, and seem to be most of them healthy and strong.' So if they are all to live without working anyway, it would be better for the State to keep them. 'But most men will laugh to hear us suppose, That any able to work should be kept without earning anything. But we Answer, That if there be but a certain proportion of work to be done, and that the same be already done by the *non-beggars*, then to imploy the *Beggars* about it, will but transfer the want from one hand to another' (Hull, 1899, vol. II, pp. 353–4).

In Chapter 2, I quoted D'Avenant who described the mysterious occurrence of what we now call depressions in terms similar to those later used by Marshall. Boisguillebert also anticipated Mill and Marshall in pointing to what seemed a very obvious fact: that circulation would be disrupted when people postponed the expenditure of their income. The growth of affluence accentuated this danger, for the purchase of luxuries could more easily be postponed (Routh, 1975, pp. 56–60).

The Physiocrats, in 18th century France, extolled the qualities of the natural order but also warned of its delicacy. François Quesnay, Court doctor at Versailles, wrote 'In the case of everything in this world, abuse is a close neighbour of order'. He warned of the danger of interruptions in the flow of spending. 'The proprietors are useful to the state only through their consumption', a proposition elaborated in his maxim, 'That the proprietors and those engaged in remunerative occupations are not led by any anxiety, unforseen by the government, to give themselves over to sterile saving, which would deduct from circulation and distribution a portion of their revenue or gains' (Routh, 1975, pp. 74–6).

One of the great paradoxes of economic thought is Malthus's recommendation of 'unproductive expenditure', while his doctrine of population condemned the mass of mankind to a life of misery. But twenty-two years after the famous *Essay* had first appeared, his *Principles of Political Economy* (1820) showed that his insights into economics had been extended and enriched. His correspondence with Senior on population shows him unrepentant, so it is surprising to find him attributing the depression of the post-Napoleonic years to a deficiency of demand. Demand stimulated invention, production and the employment of capital. But where was it to come from? The capitalists had the power but not the will to consume, and their workers had the will but lacked the power. If wages were raised, profits would fall. With some justice he observes, 'No one will ever employ capital merely for the sake of the demand occasioned by those who work for him. Unless they produce an excess of value above what they consume . . . it is quite obvious that his capital will not be employed in maintaining them' (Malthus, 1836, p. 404).

The solution lay in the demand of 'unproductive labourers' – those who did not produce a profit for their employers: menial servants, statesmen, soldiers, judges, lawyers, physicians, surgeons, clergy. Would this increase a country's wealth? Yes, for 'the motive to accumulate may be checked or destroyed by the want of effective demand long before it is checked by the difficulty of procuring the subsistence of the labourer' (ibid. p. 407).

Ricardo and Say believed firmly in the capacity of the economic system to self-adjust and insisted on the virtues of parsimony, to which Malthus rejoined: 'is it not almost a contradiction, to quote with approbation that passage of Adam Smith which says that the demand for food is limited by the narrow capacity of the human stomach, but that demand for luxuries and conveniences has no limits, and yet to say that parsimony, or the savings of expenditure in luxuries and conveniences and increasing the production of necessaries cannot be unfavourable to wealth' (Sraffa, 1962, vol. IX, p. 19).

Since the days of the Mercantilists, who recommended a country to accumulate gold, economists had over-reacted by thinking in terms of goods rather than money, so Malthus hides in a footnote an idea we have already met in Boisguillebert:

Theoretical writers in Political Economy, from the fear of appearing to attach too much importance to money, have perhaps been too apt to throw it out of their consideration in their reasonings. It is an abstract truth that we want commodities, not money. But, in reality, no commodity for which it is possible to sell our goods at once, can be an adequate substitute for a circulating medium, and enable us in the same manner to provide for children, to purchase an estate, or to command labour and provisions a year or two hence. . . . The circulating medium bears so important a part in the distribution of wealth, and the encouragement of industry, that it is hardly ever safe to set it aside in our reasonings.   (Malthus, 1836, p. 324)

Sismondi, too, asserted the existence of a 'general glut'. Since Europe had an output superior to its needs he suggested (like the Brandt Commission of our own day) that aid should be given to '*les nations barbares*'. The extension of comfort, security and welfare to these nations was a statesman's most noble wish. He gives a graphic account of the world-wide depression that 'impels the merchants in crowds to every new market, and exposes them by turns to ruinous losses, in every branch of commerce from which they looked for profit' (Sismondi, 1971, pp. 265–6).

Sismondi presents the dangers of boom and slump, inflation and deflation (without using those terms): 'nations incur dangers that seem incompatible: they fall into ruin equally by spending too much, and by spending too little. A nation spends too much whenever it exceeds its revenue, because it cannot do so except by encroaching on its capital, and thus diminishing future production. . . . A nation spends too little, whenever. . . . it does not consume the excess of its production above its exportation' (*Edinburgh Encyclopaedia*, 1830 ed., pp. 44–5).

If he could obtain those changes in the law that he wished, Sismondi asserts, he would seek only the means of assuring to those who worked the fruits of their labours (Sismondi, 1971, p. 364), but he does not tell us how this should be done. What he did do is to emphasise the dangers of the logical abstractions favoured by Ricardo and his disciples, and the importance of focusing on the problems of the real world instead of assuming they did not exist.

I have referred as paradoxical to Malthus's simultaneous adherence to contradictory ideas. John Stuart Mill (1806–73) surpasses him, arguing eloquently in favour of one proposition, which on the next page he will argue just as eloquently against. This he does in his essay 'Of the influence of consumption on production' in his youthful but brilliant little book, *Essays on some Unsettled Questions of Political Economy*.

He begins with a resounding exposition of Say's Law (though not calling it that) and a thorough trouncing of those idiots who dispute it. He spends the next dozen pages beating about the bush, and then demonstrates the extreme limitations to which Say's Law is subject. This was evidently founded on the supposition of a state of barter, but if money is used 'these propositions cease to be exactly true'. 'Now the effect of the employment of money, and even the utility of it, is, that it enables this one act of interchange to be divided into two separate acts or operations; one of which may be performed now, and the other a year hence, or whenever it shall be most convenient.' There might well be, at a given time, 'a very general inclination to sell with as little delay as possible, accompanied with an equally general inclination to defer all purchases as long as possible. . . .' Thus, 'commodities of all kinds remain for a long time unsold, and those which find an immediate market, do so at a very low price. . . . There is stagnation to those who are not obliged to sell, and distress to those who are' (Mill, 1844, pp. 69–71).

Mill beautifully describes the oscillations of the business world, where decisions have often to be made in a state of ignorance and uncertainty: 'In the present state of the commercial world, mercantile transactions being carried on upon an immense scale, but the remote causes of fluctuations in prices being very little understood, so that unreasonable hopes and unreasonable fears alternately rule with tyrannical sway over the minds of a majority of the mercantile public; general eagerness to buy and general reluctance to buy, succeed one another in a manner more or less marked, at brief intervals. Except during short periods of transition, there is almost always either great briskness of business or great stagnation; either the principal producers of almost all the leading articles of industry have as many orders as they can possibly execute, or the dealers in almost all commodities have their warehouses full of unsold goods' (Mill, 1844, p. 68).

Strangely enough, when Mill's *Principles of Political Economy* was published, four years later, supply once more creates its own demand and general gluts are once more impossible. Of the brilliant heresies of *Some Unsettled Questions* we hear no more.

3.3.1 The Empiricists

Marx designates Mill's output as 'a shallow syncretism', and the Oxford Dictionary defines 'syncretism' as 'Attempted union or reconciliation of diverse or opposite tenets or practices, esp. in philosophy or religion'. That seems an appropriate term, though I am not sure about 'shallow'. Perhaps 'bold', or even 'flagrant'. But the two streams of economics did not tend to converge. Jevons led the way into marginalism, which led Walter Bagehot, banker and editor of *The Economist*, to observe that anyone who thought what was already taught was too unlike life and business 'had better try the new doctrine, which he will find to be much worse on these points than the old' (Routh, 1975, p. 11). Economists had never been very keen on empirical research, for why bother if one were allowed to reach one's desired conclusions by making assumptions about what one did not know?

But in the course of the 19th century there came a succession of economists who insisted on the need for the patient collection of data and the study of economics as part of an historical process. Richard Jones, an early Cambridge economist who succeeded Malthus in the Chair of Political Economy at the East India Company's college at Haileybury, was of this persuasion. He warned, 'And, gentlemen, if we will not take this trouble; if we will be closet philosophers, take a peep out of our little window, and fashion a world of our own after the pattern of what we see thence, however ingenious and clever we may be, we run a risk of being sadly mistaken, and are sure to remain extremely ignorant' (Whewell, 1859, p. 570).

The marginalists were preoccupied with mathematical refinements in a world of imagination. Thomas Edward Cliffe Leslie, professor at Queen's College, Belfast, was one of the most articulate critics of their '*a priori* deductive' school. 'Instead of the world of light, order, equality, and perfect organization, which orthodox political economy postulates, the commercial world is . . . one of obscurity, confusion, haphazard, in which, amid much destruction and waste, there is by no means always a survival of the fittest, even though cunning be counted among the conditions of fitness' (Leslie, 1888, p. 235). 'Two conclusions at least, it is hoped, many readers will concur in – that the economic world is still, in a great measure, an unknown one; and that to know it economists must explore it, as geographers have explored the world of physical geography'.

3.4 THE PURSUIT OF THE TRADE CYCLE

3.4.1 Marx

Of course, if you are satisfied your pet system is perfect, you will not waste time in looking for its faults. Karl Marx (1818–83) followed a chain of reasoning that led to the opposite conclusion: that the capitalist system was fatally flawed; that its inner contradictions would inevitably lead to its own destruction. Like Richard Jones and Cliffe Leslie, he supported the historical approach, but from Hegel recruited the belief that history followed a dialectical progress powered by conflict, in which *quantitive* change built up into *qualitative* change at the height of which an oppressed class overthrew its oppressors. In philosophy he began with Hegel; in economics, Ricardo. But while Ricardo predicted the end of capitalist growth in the stagnation of the stationary state, in which profit would disappear, wages sink to the subsistence level and the whole surplus go to the landlords, in Marx capitalism was destroyed by a final crisis, and from its ruins a new system arose – that of socialism.

Marx observed the accumulation of wealth and the spread of poverty in Victorian England, and very sensibly devised a system to account for these phenomena. Cliffe Leslie and the young Mill described a world of haphazard, ruled by unreasonable hopes and unreasonable fears, and Marx, I am sure, would have agreed. But he found Ricardo's determinism irresistible and proceeded to construct a determinate system of his own. (I use the term 'system' rather than 'model' because in those days economists thought they were describing what really hapened. It was only later, when proved wrong, that they adopted the term 'model' to avoid having to discard their theories.)

But while Ricardo argued that, if workers were thrown out of employment, adjustments of wages would rapidly restore the state of equilibrium, Marx argued that unemployment was an essential ingredient of the system, the reserve army of the unemployed an indispensable adjunct of bourgeois society. This society could be understood only when economics, politics, culture and civilisation were viewed as dependent elements of an historical process. In the *Manifesto of the Communist Party* (1848), Marx and Engels present their case. Bourgeois society had conjured up gigantic means of production and exchange, but was no longer able to control them.

It is enough to mention the commercial crises that by their periodical return put on its trial, each time more threateningly, the existence of the entire bourgeois society . . . In these crises there breaks out an epidemic that, in all earlier epochs, would have seemed an absurdity – the epidemic of over-production . . . And how does the bourgeoisie get over these crises? On the one hand by enforced destruction of a mass of productive forces; on the other by the conquest of new markets, and by the more thorough exploitation of old ones. That is to say, by paving the way for more extensive and destructive crises, and by diminishing the means whereby crises are prevented.   (Marx and Engels, 1848, pp. 39–41)

In *Capital, a Critical Analysis of Capitalist Production*, Marx seeks the causes of these self-destructive activities. There were two sorts of capital: constant capital (the buildings and machinery required for production), and variable capital (the funds out of which workers were hired and wages paid). But in terms of the labour theory of value, surplus value or profit was made only on the latter. Commodities exchanged in proportion to the socially necessary labour time taken for their production. This applied not only to goods, but also to labour itself, so that the price of labour (wages) was enough only for the maintenance and reproduction of workers – a subsistence wage. If a day's subsistence required five hours work but the worker worked for ten, then the product of the additional five hours would be expropriated as the employer's profit.

But with the advance of technology, an expanding proportion of capital became tied up in constant capital (constant because it did not increase itself by returning a profit), and a falling proportion in variable capital, the base upon which profit was made. Hence a tendency for the rate of profit to fall.

And yet the intensity of competition required unceasing efforts at technological advance: a firm that fell behind would perish. But technological advance creates surplus labour. 'It forms a disposable industrial reserve army, that belongs to capital quite as absolutely as if the latter had bred it at its own cost'. Capital frantically seeks new outlets, and requires reserves of labour that may be thrown suddenly on the decisive points without injury to the scale of production in other spheres. The decennial cycle of production 'depends on the constant formation, the greater or less absorption, and the re-formation of the industrial reserve army' (Marx, 1961, pp. 631–3).

Marx searched assiduously for the formula by which capitalist crises were generated or by which they might be predicted, but never succeeded in finding it. Those who seek a lucid arrangement of Marx's economic analysis will find it in Robert Freedman, ed, *Marx on Economics* (Penguin Books, 1962).

3.4.2   The Pursuit of the Trade Cycle

Cliffe Leslie died in 1882, Karl Marx and Arnold Toynbee in 1883 (Toynbee, brightest of the Oxford economists of his generation, at the age of thirty-one). A few years later the threat to the orthodox, '*a priori* deductive' school was virtually at an end. Alfred Marshall, with his massive *Principles of Economics* (1890) and his Cambridge chair, had achieved an impregnable position. At about this time, J. A. Hobson (1858–1940) gave up his job as school teacher to seek work as a University Extension Lecturer in Economics and Literature. Unfortunately for the realisation of his hopes, he had in 1889 collaborated in a book entitled *The Physiology of Industry* in which it was argued that unemployment was caused by over-saving (a doctrine that we have traced back to Boisguillebert). 'The first shock came in a refusal of the London Extension Board to allow me to offer courses of Political Economy. This was due, I learned, to the intervention of an Economic Professor who had read my book and considered it in rationality as equivalent to an attempt to prove the flatness of the earth' (Keynes, 1936, pp. 365–6).

But while the faithful dismissed business cycles as due to natural causes, like sun-spots, or the perversity of businessmen or governments, there were others who identified them as the greatest economic evil of the age and went out to hunt them down. In this, Hobson was followed by Wesley Clair Mitchell (1874–1948) and William Henry Beveridge (1879–1963).

Hobson and his collaborator (A. F. Mummery) argued that production was reduced far below its maximum 'by the check that undue saving and the consequent accumulation of over-supply exerts on production; i.e. that in the normal state of modern industrial Communities, consumption limits production and not production consumption' (Keynes, 1936, p. 368).

Hobson is best known for his book *Imperialism, a Study*, that so impressed Lenin when it was first published in 1902, but his major preoccupation was with unemployment: *The Problem of the Unemployed* (1896, revised 1904) and *The Economics of Unemployment* (1922). He also devoted a chapter to unemployment in his major text, *The Industrial System, an Inquiry into Earned and*

Unearned Income (1909). In this chapter, he presents a succinct statement of his hypothesis:

> if the aggregate income of Great Britain were taken as £2 000 000 000 per annum, this representing the payments made to all the owners of factors of production, it could not be a matter of indifference for the future volume of production whether £300 000 000 or £400 000 000 were saved. For if £300 000 000, saved and invested in new forms of capital, provided adequately for the increased demand for final commodities which the rising consumption of the growing population will create in the calculable future, maintaining full employment for the factors of production, an attempt to save and apply to productive purposes £400 000 000 out of the same aggregate income would be an excess of saving that would defeat its purpose, creating more forms of capital than were wanted and than would actually be used.   (Hobson, 1909, p. 283)

This brings out the difference between his and Keynes's analysis rather well. Hobson, rather inconsistently in view of his other ideas, seems to take final demand as in some way objectively determined by 'the rising consumption of the growing population'. It was savings *and investment* in excess of this that caused the trouble. Keynes, however, argued (with reason) that investment itself generated incomes and demand, and that it was savings in excess of investment that resulted in deficient demand. We shall return to this when we consider Keynes later in this chapter.

For a remedy, Hobson recommended progressive taxation by which income would be redistributed from the rich to the poor: 'there can be no real remedy except a removal of the surplus elements in large incomes which brought about the disproportion between saving and spending' (Hobson, 1922, p. 148).

Beveridge and Mitchell devoted many years of their lives to the study of unemployment, each publishing the first editions of their works on that subject before the First World War. The second, much expanded, edition of Mitchell's book, *Business Cycles, The Problem and Its Setting*, appeared in 1927, after years of painstaking work at the National Bureau of Economic Research in New York.

He reviews an immense variety of theories. Jevons traced business cycles back to sun-spots that affected the weather and hence crops and prices. He found an average length of 10.466 years for the commercial cycles in the years 1821 to 1878, and 10.45 years for the sun-spot cycle. His correlation was upset, however, when astronomers revised their computations (Mitchell, 1927, pp. 12–13). Irving Fisher denied the existence of the business cycle: business simply fluctuated above and below its trend, like any other statistical series (ibid. p. 465).

Mitchell identified ten types of theory, and patiently assembled statistical data against which to view them. Most of them have faded away; none is convincing, for their proponents are often monomaniacs who assert the dominance of their pet formula. 'Read one after another in full detail, these theories are scarcely less confusing than are the commercial reviews' (Mitchell, 1927, p. 459).

However, some of those current in the 1920s are worth considering because they reappear in the 1980s. Charles O. Hardy emphasised the role of uncertainty (on which Keynes, post-1936, placed increasing emphasis). The future is judged by the present, and if the present is favourable, businessmen, making independent decisions, will over-react. 'When the increase in buying takes place it swells the volume of orders and creates a false appearance of expansion in the market, and whenever the excess stock is utilized it again gives a false indication, this time of contraction in the market' (Mitchell, 1927, p. 17).

We have noticed references to business psychology in D'Avenant, Mill, Cliffe Leslie and Marshall. Here we find it again stressed, this time by Professor A. C. Pigou, Marshall's successor at Cambridge. 'Optimistic error and pessimistic error, when discovered, give birth to one another in an endless chain'. But why do these errors not cancel themselves out? Because, once started, reactions between different parts of the business community lead the sentiment to spread and grow, since there exists between businessmen a certain measure of psychological interdependence. 'A change of tone in one part of the business world diffuses itself, in a quite unreasoning manner, over other and wholly disconnected parts'. But in addition, 'an error of optimism on the part of one group of business men itself creates a justification for some improved expectation on the part of other groups'. 'Professor Pigou represents waves of elation and depression as arising from changes in the business situation, changes which are magnified into business cycles by the emotions they excite' (Mitchell, 1927, pp. 17–19).

Most theories regarded money and bank credit as 'simply mechanisms through which the economic forces causing business cycles work their effects'. But a distinct variety of theories regarded money and banking as the source of business cycles. Alvin H. Hansen reasoned that the extension of bank credit raised prices, thus reducing the purchasing power of consumers while raising that of entrepreneurs. Business expansion ends when bank credit can no longer be extended because it has reached the limit of banking safety. R. G. Hawtrey argued along somewhat similar lines, but accounted for the cyclical movements by changes in interest rates (ibid. pp. 31–4).

Mitchell comes to the disappointing conclusion that the theories do not fit the facts. 'For the cycles explained by economic theorists are not the cycles recorded by business historians. Interested in establishing generalizations, a theorist passes lightly over the differences among successive cycles. . . . He contemplates an ideal, or a typical case, supposedly modeled on real cases and summing up all their really essential features'. This is all right provided the ideal construction is tested against the facts. Some theorists do this explicitly, while others no doubt think they have made adequate tests privately but 'spare their readers the heavy task of assessing their evidence' (Mitchell, 1927, p. 461).

There was still a long way to go, a search to understand a complex of recurrent fluctuations in numerous interrelated processes. We must learn what we can about these processes, and then see if the cause of business cycles can be identified (ibid. p. 470).

Mitchell warns of what not to do in the search for answers. An erroneous idea was present in many theories: that business cycles represent an alternate rupture and restoration of economic equilibrium. This is not the point of departure that he has chosen, so it is not his task to try to reconcile business fluctuations with the general theory of equilibrium, nor to try to reconcile that theory with facts (Mitchell, 1923, p. 462).

Like Mitchell, Beveridge assembled the statistics and sorted through the theories. In 1909, his findings on 'cyclical fluctuations' were no less disappointing. 'The causes of this fluctuation are obscure, but, beyond question, deeply seated. They are at work in all industrial countries. . . . They probably cannot be eliminated without an entire reconstruction of the industrial order. . . . Within the range of practical politics no cure . . . can be hoped for; the aim must be palliation' (Beveridge, 1930, p. 67).

The official acceptance of the need for national insurance, and the implementation, in 1911, of the National Insurance Act were advances with which Beveridge was closely associated. Palliatives were provided, but after the first World War unemployment and insecurity of employment grew still worse. The 1930 edition of Beveridge's book shows little advance in understanding. Counter-cyclical policies were under discussion, involving public works and other forms of expenditure to alleviate unemployment, but the idea was dismissed by Churchill, Chancellor of the Exchequer in 1929, though urged by, among others, Keynes and Professor Pigou. Beveridge, too, adds his voice.

One common feature of cyclical trade depressions 'was stagnation continuing in face of a low bank rate, private enterprise refusing to be roused by any amount of cheap money, dealers and manufacturers still paralysed by fear of further fall of prices and of making losses. . . . In such circumstances public enterprise, making for use rather than for sale at a profit and thus not cowed by the same fears, might lead to creation of credit that would not otherwise have come into being' (Beveridge, 1930, pp. 413–15).

But having made this practical proposal, he unexpectedly calls in the theory of marginal productivity, with its curious idea that marginal costs (the cost of producing one more unit) can be reduced by reducing output. Prices have fallen, but not money wages; so *real* wages have risen so that marginal cost is above marginal revenue. Equilibrium must be sought by dismissing workers or lowering wages. Beveridge goes along with this reasoning, but argues for increasing productivity rather than cutting wages. This requires a standstill in wages and co-operation from workers and their leaders in improving technique and organisation, as well as mobility for those workers displaced (Beveridge, 1930, pp. 416–18).

3.4.3 Keynes's Revolution

The depression of the 1930s transformed a quarter or a third of the populations of Europe and North America back in time to the state of an Indian or African village whose harvest had failed. Those who kept their jobs were better off because prices had fallen more than incomes, but were assailed by fears of losing them. The existence of bourgeois society was once more on trial. Masses of 'surplus' agricultural products were destroyed while millions of unemployed workers and their families went hungry.

Bourgeois democracy was threatened from left and right, and the teachers of bourgeois economics a bit embarrassed because what they taught was impossible had come to pass. The Marxists gloated and said, 'We told you so', and so, of course, they had. Classes sprang up, in and out of universities, to study the works of Marx.

By the introduction, in 1933, of imperfect or monopolistic

competition, Joan Robinson and E. H. Chamberlin had salvaged orthodox economics from the fancies of perfect competition; who was to save it from Say's Law? John Maynard Keynes (1883–1946) was eminently suited for this role. His teachers at Cambridge had been Alfred Marshall and A. C. Pigou, two of the most distinguished economists of the age. He himself taught at Cambridge after two years in the India Office. From 1915 to 1919, he served at the Treasury, who sent him as their representative to the Peace Conference at Versailles. His polemic, *The Economic Consequence of the Peace*, brought him world-wide fame. Then back to Cambridge to exercise his intellectual gifts as thinker, teacher, editor and adviser, a man of implacable self-confidence whose self-esteem, as Joan Robinson remarked, required no nourishment from without. (On his life and thought, see Lekachman, 1967, and Skidelsky, 1983.)

Keynes's great book, *The General Theory of Employment Interest and Money*, was published in 1936. Why the *general* theory? Because 'the postulates of the classical theory are applicable to a special case only and not to the general case, the situation which it assumes being a limiting point of the possible positions of equilibrium. Moreover, the characteristics of the special case assumed by the classical theory happen not to be those of the economic society in which we actually live, with the result that its teaching is misleading and disastrous if we attempt to apply it to the facts of experience' (Keynes, 1936, p. 3).

The book astonished the world. Here at last was a distinguished economist who was prepared to confront real problems and who spoke with all the assurance of someone who knew what he was talking about. There was tumult in the economics departments. Everyone had to pretend that they knew what Keynes meant and to take sides. And yet you will find most of the ingredients of the new theory in the old theories that we have already surveyed. Keynes acknowledged the influence of some of these theories in his Chapter 23, 'Notes on mercantilism . . . and theories of underconsumption'. He particularly admired Bernard Mandeville's *Fable of the Bees* (1723), Hobson and Mummery (1889) and Malthus (1836). Keynes was already grappling with these problems in 1930, when he published *A Treatise on Money*: 'Indeed the fact of fluctuations in the volume of fixed investment and their correlates with the Credit Cycle has long been familiar. . . . Whilst – if my theory is right – these solutions have been incomplete . . . most of them, even when they have appeared to reach opposite results, seem to me to have had hold of some part of the truth' (Keynes, 1930, vol. II, pp. 99–100).

Strangely enough, the General Theory has very few moving parts, and puts them into a simple mechanism. As Joan Robinson said, what made it 'so hard to accept was not its intellectual content, which in a calm mood can easily be mastered, but its shocking implications'. Mandeville had been impugned by the Middlesex Magistrates for proclaiming that private vices of thriftlessness were public benefits, but 'it seemed that the new doctrine was the still more disconcerting proposition that private virtues (of thriftness and careful husbandry) were public vices' (Robinson, 1962, p. 73).

Keynes explained the essence of the *General Theory* in two pages (Keynes, 1936, pp. 28–30). I present it, for easier consumption, with the symbols converted into words.

1. Technique, resources and costs of production are taken as given. Money income and real income now vary with the volume of employment.
2. What proportion of their income will the community spend on consumption? The more they get, the more they spend, but in what *proportion* depends on their psychological *propensity to consume*. If for convenience it is assumed that they spend a predetermined proportion, then consumption will vary with the level of total income which, from proposition 1, depends on the volume of employment.
3. Who decides the volume of employment? The entrepreneurs. (*Entrepreneur* is French for 'undertaker'. In English, it just means 'employer'.) They decide how many workers to employ in accordance with the amount of the resulting produce they think they can profitably sell. This is divided into two: the amount that the community is expected to spend on consumption, and the amount that it is expected will be devoted to new investment. Together, they constitute what Keynes calls *effective demand*. Note that it exists only in the minds of the entrepreneurs. It is called *effective* demand because it is their state of mind that causes them to give effect to decisions to employ.
4. Given the propensity to consume, the amount actually consumed (still all in the mind of the collective entrepreneurs) will depend on income that (from 1) depends on the volume of employment. Then what will determine the amount of expenditure on new investment? The income generated by total expenditure (total employment) *minus* the income generated by consumption (all in the minds of the entrepreneurs).

5.   Hence the volume of employment in equilibrium depends on how much entrepreneurs decide to supply, which depends on what they think the community will consume plus what they anticipate will be spent on new investment.

Now there are some important ancillary components that have to be meshed in. You will observe that all the relations postulated above are tautological: true because of the way they are defined. All the magnitudes are composed of estimates or expectations present in the minds of the entrepreneurs, whose decisions determine the volume of employment. It is in their minds that equilibrium must be established, where what they elect to supply is exactly balanced by what they imagine they can sell.

Now Keynes stipulates what it is that determines the real wage: the marginal productivity of labour in the wage-goods industries. These are the industries that produce consumer goods. He accepted, from orthodox theory, that employment will be pushed (or reduced) to that point where the marginal product of labour is equal to the wage paid. With diminishing returns (a necessary but dubious assumption) the marginal product falls as employment rises and rises as employment falls, so that it is always possible to equate the wage with the marginal product. You cannot employ more workers than are willing to work, which translated into jargon, states that the upward limit of employment is that point at which the real wage falls to equality with the marginal disutility of labour. Below this, the wage no longer compensates for the disagreeableness of having to work and the worker exclaims, 'What! Work for that wage? Not me'. (I am of course, paraphrasing Keynes.)

Next step: when employment (income) increases, the demand for consumer goods will increase too, but not by so much. So, if equilibrium is to be maintained, the sale of producer (investment) goods will have to increase *more than proportionately*. 'If the propensity to consume and the rate of new investment result in a deficient effective demand, the actual level of employment will fall short of the supply of labour potentially available at the existing real wage, and the equilibrium real wage will be *greater* than the marginal disutility of the equilbrium level of employment' (Keynes, 1936, p. 30).

Poor communities consume by far the greater part of their output, so shortfalls in demand are much smaller than in the case of rich communities. If in a rich community the inducement to invest is weak, then its output may have to fall until the surplus of its output over its consumption is sufficiently diminished to correspond to what investors are willing to invest.

Two final control mechanisms have to be introduced and then the model is complete. The *Marginal Efficiency of Capital* is the return entrepreneurs believe they can make on one more unit of investment; the *Rate of Interest* is what they would have to pay to induce owners of funds to lend them to them. Lending money involves risk and the surrender of liquidity, and we know that in certain circumstances owners of funds would rather stick to them and forgo interest rather than lend them out.

Now let us give the model a run. Day breaks and entrepreneurs are faced with the problem of how much employment to offer. Although a multitude of decisions about investment have to be made, none of them is going to make any difference to techniques or productivity *today*. Each entrepreneur says to himself, 'I will employ just that number of workers that will enable me to maximise my profits, so that if I employ one more or one less, my profits will be reduced. Some of my output will be marketed today, some tomorrow, some next week, month, year, some in years to come. What will my marginal unit of output sell for when it comes to market? Will this be greater or smaller or just equal to my costs including the interest payment that I will have to make on the funds so tied up?' Every rise or fall in interest will contract or extend the investments that it will be profitable to make.

Now, having made all the necessary calculations and taken all the possibilities into account, the entrepreneur decides how many workers to employ, and work begins.

Keynes drew two important deductions from his theory. One was that saving always equals investment, so that whatever the level of activity the system will always be in equilibrium; the other that employment could not be increased by a reduction of money wage rates, and any attempt to do so would be frustrated.

On the equality of savings and investment, he reasoned thus.

Income = consumption + investment.
Saving = that part of income not spent on consumption.
Therefore income − consumption = investment = saving.

This simple statement caused enormous confusion, for its unstated assumption was that all this occurred instantaneously. Once time is admitted, planned (or *ex ante*) saving may be very different from planned (or *ex ante*) investment. They are, in fact, unlikely to conform, and this is a matter of great importance in the actual behaviour of the economy. Bertil Ohlin explained this lucidly in Ohlin, 1950.

Of more immediate interest for our purposes was Keynes's refutation of the proposition that unemployment could always be eliminated if workers were prepared to accept the appropriate reductions in their wages. The effect of such reductions depended on a number of considerations. If prices were reduced while profit, interest and rent were not, the real income of these factors would rise, and wage income be relatively reduced. The overall result would probably be to reduce the propensity to consume so that sales of consumer goods are more likely to fall than rise. If money-wages were reduced relative to those paid abroad, the favourable balance of trade might increase, since exports would rise and imports fall, but the terms of trade would deteriorate: more exports would be required for a unit of imports. Reduced money-wages would also reduce the need for cash balances for personal and business purposes and might thus reduce the rate of interest. But it would also increase the real burden of debt held by entrepreneurs: the quantity of their products needed to repay their debts. It would also cause labour troubles: 'In fact, a movement by employers to revise money-wage bargains downwards will be much more strongly resisted than a gradual and automatic lowering of real wages as a result of rising prices' (Keynes, 1936, pp. 260–69).

The upshot of all this is that wage reductions do not present a formula for reducing unemployment. Unemployment cannot be regarded as a matter of choice on the part of those who suffer it: the existence of *involuntary* unemployment is established.

In his 'Concluding Notes' Keynes expounds the social implications of his theory. Inequality of income and wealth can safely be reduced and the propensity to consume thus increased (for the rich consume a lower proportion of their income than the poor). Far from this curbing investment, the inducement to invest is likely to be increased. Effective saving (that saving that is not denuded by unexpected losses) is determined by the scale of investment, and as capital increases, the rate of interest is likely to fall steadily until it virtually disappears. The outcome would be the 'euthanasia of the rentier' (one who lives on investment income) and consequently, 'the euthanasia of the cumulative oppressive power of the capitalist to exploit the scarcity-value of capital' (Keynes, 1936, pp. 374–7).

Running through the book is the theme of the importance of public investment as an antidote to unemployment, with echoes of Sir

William Petty in the forms that it might take. But his proposals have an added ingredient of some importance, involving the *multiplier*. Where (as today) there is idle manpower of all grades, spare capacity in factories, transport facilities and power supply and surplus raw materials, an injection of additional expenditure will spread through the economy so that the rise in output will be a multiple of the initial injection. The size of the multiplier depends on the *marginal propensity to consume*. If the ratio of the increment of consumption to the increment of income is 9:10, the marginal propensity to consume may be expressed as $1 - \frac{1}{10}$, and the multiplier = 10. Thus for every unit of new investment, ten units of expenditure will be generated and more of the spare capacity and idle resources brought into use (Keynes, 1936, p. 115).

In the preface to the *General Theory*, Keynes remarked on the difficulty of escaping from habitual modes of thought, but you may have noticed that he none the less carried over a good deal of orthodox baggage: the operational importance of 'equilibrium', the determinateness of certain economic relationships, in particular those between the rate of interest and investment, and the real wage and the marginal productivity of labour.

It may seem very difficult and confusing, but it becomes easier once one realises that Keynes himself was confused. Joan Robinson was one of his Cambridge colleagues when the *General Theory* was in process of production. Twenty-six years after its publication, she wrote, 'Keynes himself was not quite steady on his feet. His remark about the timeless multiplier is highly suspicious. And the hard core of analysis, round which his flashing controversy wheels, is based upon comparisons of static short-period equilibrium positions each with a given rate of investment going on, though it purports to trace the effect of a change in the rate of investment taking place at a moment of time' (Robinson, 1962, p. 75). In the world of economic thought, lucidity is often mistaken for simple-mindedness, and obscurity for profundity.

In the *General Theory*, Keynes employed the *a priori* deductive method, believing that the secrets of the economy could be revealed by process of logical deduction. But once his book had been released, he began a process of exploration into a world that turned out to be much more like that described by Cliffe Leslie than that of Alfred Marshall. In his paper, 'The General Theory of Unemployment' (*Quarterly Journal of Economics*, February 1937), he developed the idea of the sudden and violent changes caused by our ignorance of the future:

The practice of calmness and immobility, of certainty and security, suddenly breaks down. New fears and hopes will, without warning, take charge of human conduct. The forces of disillusion may suddenly impose a new conventional basis of valuation. All these pretty, polite techniques, made for a well-panelled board room and a nicely regulated market, are liable to collapse. At all times the vague panic fears and equally vague and unreasoned hopes are not really lulled, and lie but a little way below the surface.

Perhaps the reader feels that this general, philosophical disquisition on the behaviour of mankind is somewhat remote from the economic theory under discussion. But I think not. . . . I accuse the classical economic theory of being itself one of those pretty, polite techniques which tries to deal with the present by abstracting from the fact that we know very little about the future.

4　Contemporary Thought

4.1　INTELLECTUAL INGREDIENTS

Once more, between the economists, there is dissention. While economies flounder, colleague disputes with colleague and, in the tumult, we look back on the fifties and sixties as a golden age. Keynes's theorems had by then been assimilated. They had left much of the old teaching material intact – marginal productivity and utility, diminishing returns, equilibrium – and had presented additional material concerned with public policy, money supply and the rate of interest. The nature of interest had been redefined, savings distinguished from investment (though, *ex post*, they mysteriously coincided) and the concept of involuntary unemployment had been defined and legitimised. Teachers were thus enabled to talk plausibly about the trade cycle. And most important for their peace of mind, the methodology of economics was left undisturbed: theorising by deduction from axioms arrived at *a priori*; exemption from the tedium of empirical research.

In retrospect, the economic crises of that time seem of minor importance. Unemployment was low, inflation moderate, growth steady. Economics, it appeared, had at last come of age, and economists at last learnt how the economy could be managed, and this Treasuries and Central Banks proceeded to do. Despite the intellectual brawls of its inception, the *General Theory* had been digested without ill effect.

Thus Professor Samuelson could explain, in the 1964 edition of his textbook, 'Although much of this analysis is due to an English economist, John Maynard Keynes . . . today its broad fundamentals are increasingly accepted by economists of all schools of thought, including, it is important to notice, many who do not share Keynes' particular policy views and who differ on technical details of analysis' (Samuelson, 1964, p. 205).

Wars dragged on interminably in those years, but the battlefields were far away. There were business fluctuations in the OECD

countries, but of a minor nature. The term 'depression' was dropped
from economic commentaries as no longer applicable to the modern
world. And then, about 1972, the Devil shouted 'Ho! Let stagflation
be!' and restored the status quo.

Stagflation is a state of affairs in which stagnation coincides with
inflation, a combination impossible in the textbook model. Rising
prices should encourage production to the limit of full employment
but, after 1972, price rises accelerated, unemployment rose and output
faltered. This perverse behaviour of the real world spread confusion in
the world of ideas, and many and ingenious were the suggestions put
forward to rectify this uncomfortable state of affairs. Could the
evidence not be used to confirm rather than to refute the ruling
hypotheses? Some said, 'If the facts break the rules, then we must
change the rules; others preferred to keep the rules and change the
facts that may have been misspecified, wrongly measured or given the
wrong leads or lags.

These problems are the major preoccupation of contemporary
thought, as a prelude to which we must consider the Phillips curve and
Friedman's monetarism – that have both had a profound effect on
modern thought and policy.

4.1.1   The Phillips Curve

Phillips presented his curve in a paper published in *Economica* in
November, 1958. In his graph, the vertical axis measured the
year-to-year percentage change in wage rates, the horizontal axis the
average percentage rate of unemployment for the year. The curve
was constructed on data for the United Kingdom for the period 1861
to 1913. These are shown in Figure 4.1, each point co-ordinating level
of unemployment and change in money wage rates in each year. You
may see there, dimly represented, the silhouette of an ostrich.
Unemployment ranged from 1 to 11 per cent, wage rate changes from
− 3 to + 9 per cent. Within these ranges, practically any combination
can occur.

Phillips, however, looked at the points and saw not an ostrich but a
hyperbola. As you may know, at the one end of a hyperbola a big
change in Y goes along with a small change in X, while at the other end
a big change in X goes with a small change in Y. The equation is:

$$Y = \frac{1}{a + bX}$$

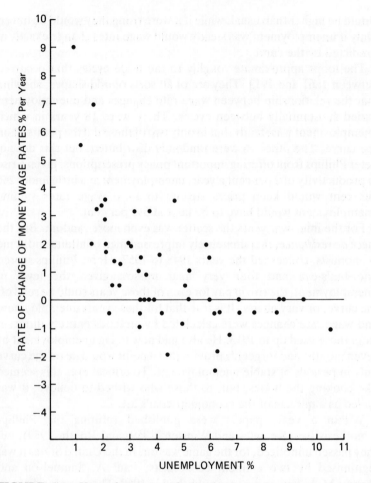

FIGURE 4.1 *Unemployment and changes in wage rates in the United Kingdom 1861–1913*

SOURCES   *see Phillips (1958)*

Once you have decided what curve you are going to fit, you do so by calculating those values of *a* and *b* that will minimise the sum of the squares of distances of each point from the curve. For details and implications, please refer to a textbook of statistics.

For various groups of consecutive years, Phillips found that the points did not sit on his curve but orbited round it, and this he explained by arguing that if in any year unemployment was falling, wage increases would be higher than usual, while if it were rising they would be lower. Only if unemployment was steady would wage rates change exactly as predicted by the curve.

The loops approximate roughly to the trade cycles that occurred between 1861 and 1913. They are of all sorts of odd shapes, showing that the relationship between wage rate changes and unemployment varied substantially between cycles. There were 18 years in which unemployment was steady, but in only two of these did the points sit on the curve. The other 16 were randomly distributed, but this did not deter Phillips from offering important policy prescriptions: given a rise in productivity of 2 per cent a year, unemployment at a little under 2½ per cent would keep prices steady; to keep wage rates steady, unemployment would have to be kept at 5½ per cent.

For the inter-war years the scatter was even more random. But the *pièce de resistance*, that immensely impressed men of affairs and some economists, concerned the years 1948 to 1957. Here, Phillips scored one bulls-eye and four very near misses: given the level of unemployment, the rise in pay for each of those years could be read off the curve, or very nearly. It is true that for these years unemployment and wage rate changes were calculated by methods entirely different from those used up to 1913. He also had now to lag unemployment by seven months and forget his proviso that a point would lie on the curve only in periods of stable unemployment. To critical eyes this seemed like cooking the books, but, to those who wished to believe, it was hailed as a miracle of the econometrician's art.

Within a year, papers were published refuting the Phillips hypothesis (see Knowles and Winsten, 1959, and Routh, 1959), but they passed unnoticed, for the game was on. In the United States it was legitimised by two eminent economists, Paul A. Samuelson and Robert M. Solow, in a paper published in 1960. Their scatter diagram was no more orderly than Phillips's, and they remarked, with justice, 'A first look at the scatter is discouraging; there are points all over the place' (Samuelson and Solow, 1960, p. 188). But they add a small additional touch of magic: the simple Phillips curve has become 'The Fundamental Phillips Schedule'. 'Clearly a careful study of this problem might pay handsome dividends' (ibid, pp. 186–7) and, indeed, much research money was dedicated to this end.

The events of the seventies demonstrated that whatever it was that controlled increases in pay, it was not the level of unemployment. In the 12 months to October 1975, average weekly wage earnings rose by 23 per cent, while numbers unemployed rose from 640 000 to

1 147 000. From October 1979 to October 1983, unemployment went from 1.4 million to 3.1 million, while earnings rose by an average of almost 12 per cent a year. Of course, the lack of correlation could have been seen by anyone who cared to examine the original statistics; now it was too obvious to be ignored, except by the most loyal and devoted minds.

4.1.2 Monetarism

Phillips's message had been a simple one: history may work its transformations, but the formula linking wage rates and unemployment is immutable. Friedman's message is equally straightforward: look after the money supply, and the economy will look after itself. The role that Phillips had ascribed to the quantity of job-seekers, Friedman ascribes to the quantity of money. If you want to explain inflation, he argues, you need look no further.

On this foundation of 'positive' economics (concerned with what *is*) Friedman builds a superstructure of 'normative economics' (concerned with what ought to be done) (Friedman, 1953, p. 3). Control of the money supply should be the beginning and end of government intervention. Competition and the free market will take care of everything else.

The quantity theory of money has been around for a long time. Sir William Petty, in the 17th century, calculated how much money was needed to operate the British economy, taking into account its 'revolutions and circulations' (Routh, 1975, p. 43). In fact, it is not actually a theory but an identity or tautology. Over any given period of time $MV = PQ$. Money times velocity of circulation equals price times quantity. In Petty's day money meant gold and silver coin. Nowadays it consists of notes and coin in circulation plus demand deposits with the banks (M_1). Add in time deposits (for whose withdrawal notice must be given) and United Kingdom residents' deposits in currencies other than sterling, and you arrive at M_3. Plastic money and cashless transactions make the concept of money still more ethereal.

Friedman, however, remarks that the relation between substantial changes in prices and the stock of money over short periods has been observed to recur uniformly under a wide variety of circumstances: 'this uniformity is, I suspect, of the same order as many of the uniformities that form the basis of the physical sciences. . . . There is an extraordinary empirical stability and regularity to such magnitudes as income velocity that cannot but impress anyone who works extensively with monetary data' (Clower, 1969, p. 111).

Over any considerable period of years, the level of output may also be included, for its relation to the stock of money and the price level is close, regular and predictable. But this is not so over short periods, and the attempt to use monetary policy to offset short-run forces will merely introduce additional instability. Governments must confine their intervention to 'keeping the stock of money growing at a regular and steady rate, month in and month out', thus promoting economic growth and a stabler environment for individual planning and social action (Ball and Doyle, 1969, pp. 144–5).

Friedman received the Nobel Prize for Economics in 1976 and devoted his lecture of acceptance to a consideration of inflation and unemployment. Phillips had referred to unemployment and wages, but Friedman and other theorists regarded 'wages' as a proxy for prices in general, thus greatly expanding the scope of the game. Friedman explains: 'Some of us were skeptical from the outset about the validity of a stable Phillips curve, primarily on theoretical rather than empirical grounds. What mattered for employers and employees was the real wage. Contracts can be framed so as to adjust to even chronically high inflation rates, provided they are fully anticipated' (Friedman, 1977, p. 455). The natural rate of unemployment was that rate that would conform with anticipations and maintain a constant rate of inflation. Surprises, causing unanticipated inflation, will cause temporary deviations from the natural rate, but in due course perceptions will adjust to reality and employment will return to the level, in accordance with real rather than monetary factors, that prevailed before the unanticipated acceleration in aggregate nominal demand (Friedman, 1977, p. 457). The unexpected rise in nominal (money) demand will first result in a rise in employment, but once the knowledge spreads that it is only a nominal and not a real increase in demand, unemployment will return to its natural rate.

The natural-rate hypothesis included the Phillips hypothesis as a special case. But 'in its present form has not proved rich enough to explain a more recent development – a move from stagflation to slumpflation. . . . On this analysis, the present situation cannot last. It will either degenerate into hyperinflation and radical change, or institutions will adjust to a situation of chronic inflation, or governments will adopt policies that will produce a low rate of inflation and less government intervention into the fixing of prices' (Friedman, 1977, p. 470).

The empirical base of the monetarist hypothesis is no more substantial than that of the Phillips curve, but Friedman is more sophisticated in presenting his ideas, protecting them with 'immunizing stratagems' that make them proof against refutation. (Popper invented this useful term. See Blaug, 1980, p. 18.)

'Only surprises matter'. Inflation of 20 per cent a year will cause no more unemployment than a zero rate, provided that everyone anticipated it. If a specified cause does not have the predicted effect, it must be due to faulty expectations (Friedman, 1977, p. 456). But a still more effective stratagem lies in the uncertain lags postulated between changes in the rate of money growth and other variables. Friedman claims there is a consistent relationship between the quantity of money and nominal income. But it is not precise nor (in his charts) visible to the naked eye because there is a lag of about six to nine months (Friedman, 1972, p. 27). Changes in nominal income show up first in output and hardly at all in prices. The effect on prices will be seen some nine to fifteen months after the effect on income and output, 'so the total delay between a change in monetary growth and a change in the rate of inflation, averages something like 15 to 24 months'. But even allowing for these delays, 'the relation is far from perfect. There is many a slip 'twixt the monetary change and the income change'. With all these provisos it is surely a demonstration of faith rather than of positive economics when he adds, 'It follows from the propositions I have so far stated that *inflation is always and everywhere a monetary phenomenon*' (Friedman, 1972, p. 28).

4.2 CASE STUDIES OF CURRENT THEORIES

At the beginning of Chapter 1 (section 1.2) I inserted a note on methodology, offered a classification of ideas, warned of the prevalence of pet theories, and suggested a set of questions by which to test them that may be paraphrased as follows:

How does the theorist know?
Are his findings based on the identification and study of economic decision-makers?
Or are they 'plucked from the air'?
(See Phelps Brown, 1972, p. 3.)

I suggest that you apply this critical apparatus to the works that are now reviewed.

4.2.1 A Monetarist View

Monetarism reflects the 'ineluctable truth in the quantity theory' (*ineluctable*: against which it is vain to struggle): 'if you increase the supply of anything, even money, its relative value will fall sooner or later, to a larger or lesser extent' (Miller and Wood, 1982, p. 11).

Many economists blend Keynes and Friedman in an uneasy mixture, but here they are kept severely apart. The Keynesians tend to dismiss the efficiency and importance of the price system, arguing that general unemployment is caused by a deficiency in aggregate demand, which wage cuts would still further reduce.

The belief that unemployment was largely unaffected by wage rates had led to massive intervention by governments or trade unions to raise wages. People are thus prevented from working for wages that relate to the current value of their output, so that it has been made increasingly difficult for the labour market to clear (that is, arrive at wages that enable all those who want a job to find one). Instead, employees get 'choosy' about the work they are prepared to accept and employers substitute capital for labour (Miller and Wood, 1982, p. 12). The operation of the market is impeded by trade unions, wages councils, laws against race and sex discrimination, alternative incomes from social security, and the cost to employers of provisions for employment protection.

These institutions administer what Hicks (1974) called a 'fixprice' sector, under a protective covering of inflation. Inflation is cumulative and habit-forming. The 'fixes' produce a state of euphoria that is followed by withdrawal symptoms and severe depression (Hayek, 1980, p. 20). Miller and Wood criticise the Conservative government that in 1979 allowed its monetarist policies to be weakened by Keynesian influences. It failed to reduce the 'fixprice' sector, trade union privileges, council housing and other obstacles to reform. It thus ensured that the recession would go deeper and last longer (Miller and Wood, 1982, p. 13).

Lucas (1981) is quoted to show that all unemployment has both voluntary and involuntary elements: it is bad luck and hence involuntary, but it entails the refusal of current work options (however miserable) and is thus voluntary. The report of the Royal Commission of 1834 rightly stressed the ill effect of paying the idle more than the industrious. Every penny thus disposed is a bounty to indolence and vice.

Miller and Wood interpret the post-1960s statistics on

unemployment, that contain many surprises. 'The most restrictive years were 1969–70 under Wilson and Jenkins, and the most expansionary 1972–3 under Heath and Barber and 1980 under Thatcher and Howe' (ibid. p. 28). But expansion in monetary demand has increasingly passed straight through the economy into prices, with little benefit to employment or output (ibid. p. 33). The worst examples are in the public sector, 'where hundreds of millions of pounds are now spent in a straight subsidy to wages' 'In medical terms, unemployment has to be classified as iatrogenic – a disease caused by the doctor' (ibid. p. 23).

To obtain a better 'strategic indicator', of unemployment, there should be excluded from the count women, males under 25 or over 54, and those who have been out of work for less than six months. This would have reduced the official figure for unemployment in July 1981 from 2¾ million to less than half-a-million (ibid. pp. 59–63).

Miller and Wood conclude their study with prescriptions for 'Freeing the Labour Market': abolish supplementary benefit for teenagers, reduce unemployment benefit, raise the threshold of income tax and re-introduce lower rate bands, reduce national insurance contributions and the national insurance surcharge, abolish Wages Councils and Agricultural Wages Boards, abolish employment protection legislation and the employment clauses of the race and sex discrimination laws, require the Department of Employment to publish annual estimates of the 'natural rate' of unemployment, remove rent controls, and finally: abolish the wage-fixing power of trade unions, beginning with the abolition of the closed shop and the extension to unions of the Monopolies Act.

4.2.2 Unemployment Voluntary and Natural

We have already met, in Friedman, the notion of the natural rate to which unemployment tends to regress. He explained it thus: 'The "natural rate of unemployment", a term I introduced to parallel Knut Wicksell's "natural rate of interest", is not a numerical constant but depends on "real" as opposed to monetary factors – the effectiveness of the labor market, the extent of competition or monopoly, the barriers or encouragements to working in various occupations, and so on' (Friedman, 1977, p. 458).

If the government stimulates demand and drives unemployment below the natural rate, money wage rises accelerate, generating inflationary expectations with accelerating price rises (Miller and Wood, 1982, pp. 13–14). But according to Friedman, it is only *unexpected* changes in inflation that cause deviations from the natural rate of unemployment. If inflation is correctly anticipated, the 'expectations-augmented Phillips curve' will be vertical to the x-axis: that is, unemployment, depending on *real* factors, will remain constant while wage changes are determined by expectations and contracts so framed as to take account of price rises.

You may remember that Friedman, in his interpretation of the Phillips curve, substituted the rate of inflation (or price rises in general) for the rate of increase in wage rates. But Friedman wanted to attribute price rises to something else (unmerited increases in the supply of money), so had to liberate them from dependence on the level of unemployment. The natural rate of unemployment was presented as a function of a bundle of non-monetary determinants, with *changes* in that level due to faulty predictions of future price rises on the part of workers and employers.

The definition of the natural rate, to borrow a legal phrase, is vague and embarrassing, and lends itself to different interpretations. Challen, Hagger and Hardwick (1984) invoke 'the help of the important concept of the *natural unemployment percentage*, to be abbreviated henceforth by NUP. . . . The NUP is a *hypothetical* unemployment percentage; it is that unemployment percentage which *would be* observed in any period if the number of jobs on offer were equal to the number of persons wishing to hold jobs', and they define NUP as 'that unemployment percentage which would be observed in any period if the excess demand for labour were zero' (and likewise, of course, the excess supply) (ibid. p. 131).

Addison and Siebert (1979) give a concise exposition of how the system is supposed to work:

> In the Friedman model, there is a natural rate of unemployment consistent with any of a wide variety of steady rates of inflation or deflation, as determined by the rate of growth of the money supply. This natural rate of unemployment is determined by such factors as the costs of gathering information about job vacancies in a given market. . . . It is possible to reduce unemployment temporarily below the natural rate by expanding aggregate demand. But, by causing prices to rise, this lowers the real wage and induces employers to expand output and employment. At first, workers do not realize that the increase in prices has reduced their real wage.

Once this fact is recognized, however, they demand and obtain higher nominal wages and the reduction of real wages below the equilibrium level can be maintained only by a further rise in prices. As prices and wages continue to rise at a steady rate, workers eventually come to anticipate the price increases and to act on their anticipations. Accordingly, in the course of time, real wages and employment fall back to their equilibrium levels and unemployment is restored to the natural rate. . . . Attempts to maintain a level of unemployment below the natural rate imply an accelerating rise in prices. (Addison and Siebert, 1979, p. 426)

The natural rate of unemployment can thus prevail through price increases of any magnitude provided these increases are fully anticipated. But unanticipated price changes (caused by 'shocks') reactivate Phillips curves (with parameters that are not predetermined) so that rising unemployment may be associated with rising rates of pay increase (Addison and Siebert, 1979, fig. 12.5, p. 426).

This brings us to the Expectations-augmented Phillips Curve, in terms of which the pay increase that would have been associated with the old-style Phillips curve is augmented by an allowance to compensate for the expected rate of inflation. This, in turn, leads to the theory of Rational Expectations. Friedman has asserted that the economic decision-makers (entrepreneurs and workers) are capable of rightly predicting the future course of wages and prices, or, if not, of acting as if they had. So it is that the natural rate of unemployment can co-exist with any rate of (predicted) inflation.

Joll, McKenna, McNabb and Shorey (1983) explain the reasoning thus:

If agents use current money statistics . . . to formulate price expectations they will arrive at or be induced to arrive at the wrong expectations only by unforeseen changes. . . . The government cannot bring about deviations from the natural rate, even temporarily, except by manipulating [unforeseen changes] in a totally unpredictable way: something which is at odds with governments' natural inclinations and with achieving and maintaining desired levels of unemployment . . . and any form of activist policy by the government is totally ineffective.

'Such an approach to expectations formation can be criticised in that it assumes that labour market agents have complete statistical information and knowledge of the structural relationships within the economy and the causation underlying them. . . . Such an expectations approach subsumes in workers' behaviour that they recognise that everyone will follow the same approach and reach the same conclusions. (Joll, McKenna, McNabb and Shorey, 1983, p. 351)

M. FG. Scott adds a further variation, defining the natural level of unemployment as 'that level which would suffice to stop inflation accelerating' (Blackaby, 1980, p. 11). He elaborates with commendable caution, 'If there is no money illusion, and if the Phillips curve exists, and if, in the long run, prices must rise as fast as wage costs per unit of output . . . then accelerating inflation can only be avoided by keeping unemployment at the level at which wage rates would rise as fast as labour productivity when inflation is zero. This is the natural level of unemployment' (Blackaby, 1980, p. 15). He notes much uncertainty about the magnitude of the natural level and suggests that (in June 1980) it may be higher than 5 or 6 per cent. He strays again from the monetarist fold by suggesting that, if it is, we shall have to attempt to reform the wage-fixing system, for monetary and fiscal policies are unlikely to be able to achieve the desired effect (ibid. p. 23).

Samuel Brittan (1982) also follows a path of his own. There is no set of equations that can identify and measure a trade-off between unemployment and inflation, 'because so much depends on the state of expectations, beliefs about policy, and the confidence with which the beliefs are held – as well as on unpredictable but quite frequent shocks which can knock the economy off course'. But he still seeks to know 'the rate at which unemployment will settle after inflation has fallen to the target level and various shocks, whether induced by policy or not, have worked their way out of the system' (Brittan, 1982, p. 110). What, that is, is the NAIRU? – the Non-accelerating Inflation Rate of Unemployment, what Friedman has, unfortunately in Brittan's view, called the 'natural rate'.

Pure monetarists regard all unemployment as voluntary. Brittan agrees that many of the unemployed might find work if they were willing to accept a sufficient drop in pay or change in conditions, but maintains that there is no clear dividing line between voluntary and involuntary unemployment. 'To say that real wages have diverged from market-clearing wages is a statement of the problem, not an answer. The important issue is *why* they have diverged' (Brittan, 1982, p. 117). Inflation may have contributed, but Brittan attributes more importance to the decline of manufacturing in the industrialised countries, whose costs of production are far higher than in the newly industrialising countries. Other causes were the reduction of overmanning that began in the 1980 recession, and the general rise in wage costs as a proportion of value added.

But the long-term trend in the jobs market, with its perverse upturn in real wages, is due to influences on the side of labour supply. Housing difficulties may have reduced mobility, while the poverty and unemployment trap have affected the 'reservation wage'. In November 1980, a man with children had net spending power that varied very little whether his wage was £45 or £105 a week. The fall in the real tax threshold had also affected the poverty trap: in 1955 a married man with two children paid income tax if he was on average earnings or above; in 1975 he began paying at 44 per cent of average earnings; in 1981, at 38 per cent. 'If some "desire to work" of a non-pecuniary kind did not exist it would be difficult to explain why so many low-paid bother to seek jobs' (Brittan, 1982, pp. 126–9).

T. D. Sheriff enters the list with an examination of two major types of wage equation. The expectations-augmented Phillips curve (EAP) assumes that the rate of wage inflation is determined by the demand and supply of labour plus expected future price inflation, with the wage bargain thus carried out in real terms (Blackaby, 1980, p. 214); and the target real wage hypothesis (TRWH), that follows a bargaining approach to wage determination. In the TRWH, employees want to increase their real wages by some target over time; if they fail, they will afterwards try to make up for lost ground. But Sheriff is sceptical about the stability of the parameters, for there are good reasons for believing the social and political factors outweigh the economic. He agrees with Artis (1976) that neither an EAP or a TRWH has been particularly successful in explaining money wage behaviour. The possibility of the underlying economic forces being captured econometrically, he concludes, needs to be entertained with some humility (Blackaby, 1980, p. 226).

Stephen Nickell also explores the terrain of the expectations-augumented Phillips curve. Pre-tax wages depend on expected prices, the difference between actual and equilibrium unemployment, and the rates of taxation (Nickell, March 1982, p. 52). If input prices rise faster than output prices, target post-tax real wage growth must decelerate, or unemployment will rise. But government policy in Britain since 1979 has achieved a remarkable combination of soaring unemployment and soaring real wages. Nickell despairs of finding a set of policies that will minimize unemployment and maximise real incomes in the long run. 'This we shall never know' (ibid. p. 55).

He elaborates these ideas in Nickell, September 1982, seeking to discover the determinants of equilibrium unemployment in Britain. His industry and manipulative dexterity are impressive, but in the end he admits, 'Although we have identified a number of possible important factors in this macro time series context, unless we obtain micro-economic confirmation of these results they will remain as little more that tentative conjectures' (Nickell, September 1982, p. 571).

Blackaby is sceptical of the rationality of rational expectations, that depend on the proposition that the decision-makers are heavily influenced by their expectations of future trends in the economy. These are supposed to consist not simply of the extrapolation of past trends but to take into account information about government intentions, for example the medium-term money supply targets. 'After a time, when people realise that the government is determined to adhere to these numbers, behaviour in the labour market will adjust to them. People will stop pricing themselves out of the labour market'. But there were difficulties in the application of these ideas to the labour market. They might apply to some areas, such as exchange-rate or interest-rate determination, but the bargaining process in the labour market was not one of them (Blackaby, 1980, p. 117).

You may now perceive the strong political implications of this set of theories. Gustavo Maia Gomes remarks, 'agents in economic models have become rational in so strong a sense that it is now difficult to know where rationality stops and omniscience begins. It has been a short step to develop macroeconomic models where unemployment appears as something of a logical impossibility, and where stabilization policies are proven to be ineffective' (Gomes, 1982, p. 51).

4.2.3 Do Trade Unions Cause Unemployment?

Trade unions are front-runners in the inflation stakes. One of their prime objectives is to raise the pay of their members which, in the modern world, they generally succeed in doing faster than the rise in productivity. Less than half the employed population belong to unions, and pay negotiation is a bilateral matter requiring agreement between employers and employees, but the unions appear to set the pace. They may be agents of inflation; are they also agents of unemployment?

Professor Friedrich A. Hayek emphatically answers, 'Yes!' He traces the trouble back to the Trade Disputes Act of 1906, that exempted unions from legal actions for damages inflicted on employers. This, Hayek remarks, was a bit of lunacy perpetrated by a vote-catching party. The legal privileges enjoyed by the unions are the chief causes of unemployment (though 'The final disaster we owe mainly to Lord Keynes') (Hayek, 1980, p. 57).

He warns against interference with the market. 'In the real world, nobody can know where people are required but the market, which observes and digests the myriad bits of information possessed by all who buy or sell in it'. The unions impede increases in productivity and hence the growth of real wages. They become the chief cause of unemployment (and then blame the market economy) by impeding the deployment of labour in accordance with the demand for products. To cure unemployment, workers must be redirected to jobs where they can be 'lastingly' employed. In a free society, this requires changes in relative wages to make labour-surplus occupations or industries less attractive and labour-scarcity ones more so. 'This is *the essential mechanism which alone can correct a misdirection of labour* in a society where workers are free to choose their jobs' (Hayek, 1980, p. 56).

Patrick Minford takes a somewhat similar view. His researches at the University of Liverpool indicate that wages are pushed up in the union sector, causing a loss of jobs; pay in the non-union sector is then prevented from falling to the full employment level by the joint effect of unemployment benefits and income tax, thus limiting its ability to absorb workers displaced from the union sector. The substantial rise in union power since the early 1960s has raised unemployment by about a million (Minford, 1982, p. 73). A union is like any other monopoly: it sets its price above the free competitive level and thus reduces the size of the market.

At Liverpool, wage and unemployment equations were estimated for annual data from 1955 to 1979, and quarterly data from 1964 to 1979, and a term was inserted for the unionised proportion of the labour force.

The unionisation rate in 1963 was 43 per cent; by 1979 it had risen to 56 per cent. Our estimates indicate this would have raised total real wages, once fully worked through, by 13 per cent compared with what they would otherwise have been. The effect on output would be to reduce it by 8½ per cent. The effect on the PSBR [public sector

borrowing requirement] is correspondingly severe: an increase of
£6½ bn at 1981 prices. The effect on unemployment, coming
through the increased substitution of mechanisation for labour
(about 650 000) and through the contraction of output (about
350 000), would be about 1 million.   (Minford, 1982, pp. 74–5)

The solution? 'Only changes in laws and institutions which take away
union power will remove its effects on unemployment, output and the
interests of non-unionised workers' (ibid).

Professor James Meade believes that stagflation has been induced
by the increased ability and willingness of unions (and similar
monopolistic pressure groups) to attempt to get increases in real pay in
excess of the available increases in real output, after allowing for an
acceptable profit margin. This causes reduced demand for the
products of industry, which leads to heavy and continuing
unemployment. The pressure of the unemployed may then undermine
the power of the unions, and new and lower money wage rates may
then be fixed, but the damage will have been done: the economy will
be in recession, output lower and numbers of workers involuntarily
unemployed (Meade, 1982, pp. 21–2).

Samuel Brittan takes a different view: 'if union power was the
dominant force behind continuous inflation, it would suggest that
union leaders were interested in money wages – i.e. numbers on pieces
of paper – rather than real wages. They are not so irrational.'
Monopolies cause the price of their product to be higher than
otherwise; they do not cause a continuing rise. But unions have priced
people out of work, for example by over-pricing the labour of young
people, and unemployment will get worse if union power increases or
unions make more use of their existing power. They cause 'wage
distortion', though it is difficult to know how much: perhaps 10 per
cent in the United States and between 12 and 25 per cent in Britain?
This (following the Liverpool model) would raise unemployment by
750 000. The reinforcement of union power has inhibited the efficient
functioning of the relevant markets (Brittan, 1982, pp. 130–3).

Colin Clark has been studying income and employment for more
than fifty years and is a pioneer of national accounting, so his ideas must
not be lightly dismissed. He asks, 'Do trade unions raise wages?' and
answers no. 'So blaming trade unions for inflation is wide of the mark.
As Professor Alan Walters has pointed out, even if trade unions
possessed all the power sometimes attributed to them, they could still

only organise a once-for-all wage increase, not a continuing inflation; and the power of trade unions is on the whole decreasing. . . . Blaming trade unions for inflation is to be deprecated, because it diverts attention from the fiscal and monetary policies of governments, the real offenders'. Even if trade unions ceased to exist, wages would not be very different from what they are now. Unions have some effect in adding to unemployment, mainly among the unskilled, but their real harm lies in reducing real incomes by their stubborn insistence on over-manning (Clark, 1981, pp. 228–9).

Does union power to raise wages result in the misallocation of labour? Peter Lilley is suspicious of the empirical evidence. 'The direction of causality is always ambiguous in market data. This is the regrettable consequence of the market's most desirable feature – the mutual responsiveness of everything to everything else'. He is sceptical, too, about accusations that unions misuse monopoly power. Nearly a quarter of United Kingdom output is exported, while probably an equal proportion is subject to import competition, so that in at least half the economy the labour force, whether unionised or not, is competing directly with foreign labour and has thus negligible power over the market. For their members, they serve a purpose analogous to that played by an estate agent in the sale of a house when he uses his knowledge of the market to get the best price in a desired period. The union seeks the highest wage compatible with the continued prosperity of the firm. This positive aspect should be enhanced while harmful effects are mitigated (Blackaby, 1980, pp. 61–3).

4.2.4 Social Compacts and Institutional Reform

Despite Milton Friedman's clear distinction between the two, we find that in the reasonings of the theorists the positive and the normative are inextricably mixed. Indeed, their diagnosis of what is wrong is sometimes best understood by studying their prescriptions for putting it right. Pure monetarists, believing that the economy is market-regulated, prescribe only the control of the money supply. Non-purists seek to change behaviour and regulate institutions. If, voluntarily or by changes in the law, union power can be socialised (that is, made socially benign), then perhaps Keynesian remedies might be applied without inflationary effects and damage to the balance of payments?

Much thought has been applied to this problem. The Royal

Commission on Trade Unions and Employers' Associations (the Donovan Commission) reported in 1968, and a procession of statutes has followed, with Conservative and Labour governments undoing each other's laws and recasting them nearer to their own hearts' desires (see the chapters in Bain, 1983, by Roy Lewis and Bob Hepple). There continues to be much speculation and some empirical research within this field. John Bennett, Industrial Relations Librarian at the University of Warwick, compiles an annual bibliography of relevant books and papers for the United Kingdom. That for 1982 contains 1094 items (Bennett, 1984).

The theorists whose work I now review believe that it is possible to humanise the capitalist system so that unemployment and inflation may be mitigated. That, of course, was Keynes's aim: to preserve the 'traditional advantages of individualism'. 'The authoritarian state systems of to-day seem to solve the problem of unemployment at the expense of efficiency and of freedom. It is certain that the world will not much longer tolerate the unemployment which, apart from intervals of excitement, is associated – and, in my opinion, inevitably associated – with present-day capitalistic individualism. But it may be possible by a right analysis of the problem to cure the disease whilst preserving efficiency and freedom' (Keynes, 1936, pp. 380 and 381).

James Meade presents the most ambitious plan for the attainment and preservation of full employment within the capitalist framework. The financial authorities would have the task of restraining the increase in money expenditure to about 5 per cent a year, while the Meade plan would reduce or eliminate cost inflation. The flow of labour would be controlled by variations in rates of pay, with pay rises avoided in sectors with excess labour, and promoted in those with labour shortages. Full employment could then be maintained with only minor and temporary lapses, and inflation, too, would be very moderate (Meade, 1982, p. 7).

Meade accepts the findings of OECD (1965) and Reddaway (1959) that changes in the deployment of labour have not been determined by changes in relative rates of pay, but this, he suggests, rests upon the fact that changes in relative pay have not been very marked. If they had been, they would have exerted a powerful allocative influence (Meade, 1982, pp. 89–90). Though the market does not conform with the model of perfect competition it may be made to do so (ibid. p. 43).

These objectives will be attained by a system of 'Not-Quite-Compulsory Arbitration'. Bargaining between workers and employers will continue as heretofore, but the ultimate appeal to the strike will be replaced by an ultimate appeal to an external impartial arbitral body that, in making its award, will put great emphasis on the promotion of employment (Meade, 1982, p. 108). It would not be unlawful for either side to take industrial action, even against the terms of an award, but it would be made unprofitable: a worker striking against an award would thereby terminate his contract of employment, with forfeiture of redundancy pay and no right of re-engagement. Supplementary benefits for those on strike would be by loan and strikers would get no tax refunds from PAYE. They and their unions would forfeit immunities from actions for damages. For employers, it would simply be made unlawful to employ anyone except on the terms of the award (ibid. pp. 115–16).

David Metcalf also believes that unions play a central role in the process of inflation and recommends the reform of collective bargaining. He is thus a deviant from the monetarist line, though he borrows their concepts of equilibrium unemployment, shocks and control of the money supply. Given these clues, it is possible to follow his argument:

> Reform should concentrate on the macroeconomic question of how to keep near – rather than above – the equilibrium rate of unemployment in the face of (short-run) reductions in monetary demand and (long-run) shocks. A successful pay policy represents a favourable supply shift (or shock) which reduces the price at which firms are prepared to supply a given output. So for a given growth in nominal income it would make possible a simultaneous reduction in inflation and increase in real output and employment. The authorities can then decelerate the rate of monetary growth without causing higher unemployment. (Blackaby, 1980, pp. 52–5)

But in enforcing pay policy, he supports the taxation of excessive pay increases rather than a search for voluntary agreement and co-operation.

Sir Henry Phelps Brown, too, is sceptical of the possibility of voluntary agreement, for the trend towards business unionism in Britain leaves little future for the Social Contract. (The term 'business unionism' comes from the United States, where depoliticised unions, like business enterprises, seek to maximise the income of their members.) Professor Phelps Brown reminds us that in the approach to the general election in 1978–9, unions were prepared to exercise little restraint to help the Labour government. He regards a tax on pay settlements in excess of the norm as administratively impracticable

(Blackaby, 1980, pp. 92–4). He suggests, though, that there is a positive case for convening a new type of consultative assembly representative not of trade unions and employers' associations as such, but of the principal negotiating units. Their task would be to arrive at the pay movements justified by the economic outlook, thereby separating pay regulation from industrial relations (Blackaby, 1980, pp. 97–8).

Richard Layard argues for a tax-enforced incomes policy, but it should be a tax exacted on employers who give increases in excess of the norm (Layard, 1981, pp. 17–18). He guesses that voluntary unemployment has increased because of administrative changes and the separation of offices paying benefit from job centres, whereby less pressure is put on the unemployed to find work. All the same, there are more work-hungry unemployed than there used to be. The rise in unemployment has been caused by a shortage of jobs rather than of willing workers.

As a means of expanding the demand for labour, Layard in 1976 advocated the payment of subsidies for extra jobs, and in 1977, the Small Firms Employment Subsidy was introduced. Two years later, it might have embraced nearly a quarter of a million jobs, but was then abolished by the government of the day. He suggests a subsidy of £70 a week to an employer for hiring anyone who has been unemployed for over six months, and that any worker unemployed for over six months should have the right to be employed on a publicly-supported project at a wage 10 per cent higher than his benefit entitlement (Layard, 1981, p. 14).

Hunter and Mulvey emphasise the need to take cognisance of social and institutional factors, that are of immense importance in detemining the terms on which commerce proceeds. In the labour market, their influence is probably much greater than in most commodity markets. There is in fact a complex of labour markets, in a constant state of flux, to which political as well as economic theory must be applied (Hunter and Mulvey, 1981, pp. 132–42). Professor Hunter presents a picture of the future in which governments are likely to be compelled to resort to incomes policies to induce moderation, with bargaining between union federations and governments including protectionism, quality of working life, industrial democracy (with employee investment funds as in the Heidner proposals in Sweden) and, in its most extreme form, demands for the steady replacement of the market by state ownership or control (Hunter, 1980, pp. 17–18).

Derek Robinson and Ken Mayhew accept collective bargaining as the preferred method of determining pay and conditions of employment in Britain. To an increasing extent, however, the outcome has been seen as unacceptable or contrary to the public interest, so that there is a need to apply constraints. The range of policies is constantly changing, but it may be that none is capable of reconciling the social, political and economic aspirations of groups and individuals with national economic realities. 'If this is the case the future is indeed bleak' (Robinson and Mayhew, 1983, p. 13). Mayhew demonstrates the difficulty of gauging the effect of past policies. They might at least have postponed the onset of inflation, so a case can be made for conventional incomes policies. But they must be by consent, and this is difficult to maintain or even obtain, considering the many interests involved (ibid., pp. 19–20).

William Brown asks if collective bargaining can be so structured as to make outside intervention unnecessary. Its fragmented nature has left individual groups of employees with little option but to engage in competitive over-bidding in an effort to protect their real earnings. They thereby exacerbate the inflation they individually seek to outpace. The TUC has taken advantage of the recession to co-ordinate union activities, but the task for the Confederation of British Industry is more difficult, for British managements do not see solidarity as a virtue. 'In principle it should not be too difficult to co-ordinate the 100 or so pay control points covering 10 000 or more employees. . . . In practice, lulled by a sympathetic government and subdued workforces, members see little purpose in combining' (Robinson and Mayhew, 1983, p. 58). The growth of union power was demonstrated by the rise in the number of full-time shop-stewards (who are paid by management but devote their working-hours to union duties) that between 1966 and 1976 had quadrupled to between four and five thousand, with possibly an equal number in the public sector. The number of union officials paid by union funds has not exceeded 4000, so it is evident that we have recently witnessed a fundamental change in union organisation (Blackaby, 1980, p. 143); 'without the emergence of employer solidarity there is no chance of Britain achieving coordinated collective bargaining and, consequently a long-term incomes policy' (ibid. p. 147).

Keith Sissons, too, sees the decentralised and fragmented nature of the bargaining process as the principle flaw in the British system of pay settlement. It is a major cause of disputes, especially in periods of economic decline, and promotes the upward movement of pay settlements. For this, it is sufficient if groups of workers try to keep up with settlements negotiated elsewhere; there does not have to be a recognisable key bargain nor a clear pay round. Sissons proposes a three-stage bargaining process, beginning with the government, the TUC and CBI. They would first agree on real incomes and net income after tax. Stage two would relate to the way in which pay increases should be divided, and stage three would require the negotiators in individual bargaining units to decide how they were to allocate the increases within their discretion (Blackaby, 1980, p. 101). To expect individual trade unions to exercise moderation when there was no guarantee that others would do likewise was totally unrealistic (ibid. pp. 104–5).

Of the writers reviewed above, Metcalf and Layard believe that pay restraint can be enforced by taxation; Phelps Brown and Sissons that institutional changes might be introduced; Meade that the good sense of his proposals might carry the day; the others see the need for income policies, but their hopes are tempered by doubts. It may be, as Robinson and Mayhew suggest, that the task of reconciliation is impossible. Similar problems of reconciliation confront the theorists: 'The relative merits of general economic measures *versus* institutional and attitudinal ones will continue to be debated by policy-makers and economists. That this debate will not be resolved, and indeed may be insoluble, is probably an innate part of the economic problem' (Robinson and Mayhew, 1983, p. 137).

4.2.5 Qualitative Changes?

The early Marxians, like the early Christians, believed in the imminence of the millenium. Some Christians still do, after two thousand years, and so do some Marxians after a hundred, but most people have given up. If there is to be a moral transformation, it will have to come by a lot of hard work by a lot of people, and if there is to be a social transformation, it will have to be by democratic process. The proletariat, like the law, has turned out to be a ass, submitting to exploitation in exchange for the trumpery of consumerism, puppets of the box and of the press. A violent revolution is more likely to lead to the dictatorship of mindless thugs than of the proletariat.

Marx and Engels, looking back over history, observed that progress was not guaranteed: thesis was not always overcome by antithesis to create a higher synthesis. Sometimes the struggle led to the common ruin of the contending parties (Marx and Engels, 1848, p. 33). At the end of the last section we were left in doubt as to whether it is possible to do a repair job on the capitalist system in the way that Keynes had hoped. Now we ask whether it is possible to avert common ruin by producing some sort of qualitative change that will allow public control of production and growth, and eliminate the alternative phases of mania and depression.

Adrian Sinfield names the last chapter of his book *Work for All*, but the outlook is not rosy.

> The truth is that all governments, Labour and Conservative, over the last decade and a half have presided over major increases in unemployment on a scale that would have seemed impossible or intolerable in the 1950s when 'full employment' was so complacently assumed. Both parties are well aware that they cannot simply blame world conditions. . . . Over at least the last ten years, every government has deliberately made use of some policies that they knew would increase unemployment whether to control inflation or the unions or both. . . . Yet throughout this period there has been not one major initiative to help those out of work. . . . This inaction contrasts sharply with measures introduced in many other market economies. (Sinfield, 1981, p. 148)

There is much work to be done (for example to improve housing and household equipment as well as education and other social services). Workers are available. Only the jobs remain to be created. It is necessary to plan for a society that involves all its members and actively promotes their participation in its work (ibid. p. 157). Similar arguments are advanced in Showler and Sinfield, 1981, pp. 231–3. 'Work for all' must be given political, social and economic priority. This will require effective income maintenance and manpower policies and, over all, an active employment policy. They do not present a programme of how this might be done, though they refer to the proposal contained in the *Cambridge Economic Policy Review*, 1980, calling for general import controls. They speak, too, of the promotion of exports and production of import substitutes by direct government investment (Showler and Sinfield, 1981, p. 233).

Showler and Sinfield wrote a year or two after the advent of the Conservative government of 1979; Michael Barratt Brown, Ken Coates, Ken Fleet and John Hughes a year before the fall of the Labour government. It is surprising to be reminded how little the problems and policies seem to have changed. Professor Townsend provides an overview. The challenge was already there of whom to admit to the category of unemployed, with Sir Keith Joseph and others trying to reduce the numbers by excluding the handicapped, the sick and those between jobs. 'The real problem is, however, not one of overestimation but underestimation. . . . The Census of 1971 found 400 000 more unemployed than were registered with the Department of Employment' (Barrat Brown, 1978, p. 10). The Labour movement had to choose between a weak attempt to moderate the human consequences of capitalism, or the establishment of an alternative structure of full, equitable employment for the whole population. Full employment was as much a social as an economic objective. Townsend cites Sweden as an example of what might be done. A Royal Commission on long term employment policy was set up in 1974. The Nordic countries had a common programme that included the advance of public investments and public orders for industry, stockpiling, support for training rather than lay-offs and dismissals, new recruitment in the public sector and temporary employment in relief projects in industry and service. In spite of the world recession, employment in Sweden had continued to increase (Barratt Brown, 1978, pp. 11–12).

Stuart Holland presented an alternative economic strategy, related to the changed structure of big business since the war. Thirty years ago, the 100 biggest companies supplied between a fifth and a quarter of output and employment. Now (1978) they commanded half of manufacturing output and employment and more than half British export trade. Their monopolistic power enables them to pass on the higher costs of materials from abroad, and higher interest charges and unit costs of under-utilised plant. So, the greater the deflation, the greater the rise in prices. Unit costs would be reduced if output were increased. 'Therefore, the key short to medium term policy should be a restoration of the projected reduction of public expenditure (i.e. 'reverse the cuts') plus price controls' (Barratt Brown, 1978, p. 133). Other measures would include increased expenditure by the National Enterprise Board, obligatory planning agreements between the top 100 firms, their unions and the government, and a move to joint reflation and restoration of public expenditure by the members of the EEC (ibid. p. 136).

It may be that a compromise, gradualist policy is the only politically plausible policy for Britain. This has been the line of successive Labour governments, but Tom Clarke has argued that it will not lead to a democratically planned and controlled economy. This the 'piecemeal nationalisation of previous Labour governments' failed to do. Some important industries were nationalised, but:

> invariably they were in bad condition due to neglect, their private owners were massively compensated, and they required vast investment programmes to renovate them. Profitable and growth industries were left in private hands, and so ironically nationalization *strengthened* the private sector and capitalist class. . . . No attempt was made to shift power towards the workers in the nationalized industries; rather, executive hierarchies were consciously created to rival the splendour of the private sector, with chairmen so powerful and remote that one leading figure was described as 'bossman personified: omniscient, intolerant, domineering and responsive only to the crudest flattery'. (Clarke and Clements, 1977, p. 377)

Andrew Glynn and John Harrison are also critical of Labour's 1974 Alternative Economic Strategy. 'An economic strategy for the working class should certainly include demands to keep up wages, reverse cuts and start more public works. But such measures alone would not cure the system's ailments. On the contrary, they would create further difficulties' (Glynn and Harrison, 1980, p. 151). The Alternative Economic Strategy if it really threatened the economic power of business corporations was likely to result in an 'investment strike'. 'With the government issuing directives, appointing official trustees and nationalising firms which refused to fall into line, capital's priority would be to defend its control over production. . . . It would cease investment, cut back on production, refuse to release essential stocks, ship assets abroad and whatever else it deemed necessary. The result would be economic and social chaos. Capital will not give up control over economic activity without a fight' (ibid. pp. 157–8). This is a fight that could be won only by a thorough-going socialist programme, that would require 'the broadest possible mobilisation of workers, both at home and abroad' (ibid. p. 174).

5 Assessment of Current Theories

5.1 METHODS

If at the end of Chapter 3 the theories seemed confused, at the end of Chapter 4 the confusion was surely worse confounded, the contrast of views even more bewildering. At the end of 1984, the economies of OECD countries continued to falter, with only the United States and Sweden showing clear signs of improvement. On the records of past trade cycles, improvement is long overdue. This may not be the fault of the economists, for much of their advice is ignored. But the varieties of advice tendered enable governments, as Lord Bauer observed, to select as advisers those economists that they know will advise them to do what they intend to do anyway (Bauer, 1984, p. 153).

One reason why contradictory theories are able to co-exist is the lack of rigour in the tests to which they are put in university economics departments. The theories are not theories in the scientific sense, established by practical tests, but, as I have remarked, pet theories of ornamental rather than practical purpose. They might or might not qualify for promotion if they were properly tested, but their proprietors generally do not care to expose them to such risks, and it is not expected that they should. This applies to Keynes's *'General Theory'* as much as to Friedman's monetarism or Hayek's structuralism. The great debate, that Keynes once appeared to have won, has broken out anew with battle lines little changed and facts still neglected in the way described by Beveridge in 1937. Criticism accumulates but academic economics survives unscathed, the anguished cries of the critics of the past re-echoing today: *The Crisis in Economic Theory* (Bell and Kristol, 1981), *Why Economics is not yet a Science* (Eichner, 1983), *Why Economists Disagree* (Cole, Cameron and Edwards, 1983), *Economics in Disarray* (Wiles and Routh, 1984) and *What is Political Economy?* (Whynes, 1984).

Thus most of the ideas reviewed in Chapters 3 and 4 have not got beyond the stage of hypothesis. Of the papers appearing in the *American Economic Review* from March 1977 to December 1981, Leontief observes that 54 per cent present mathematical models without any data, 11.6 per cent are non-mathematical without data, and 22.7 per cent present empirical analysis using indirect statistical inference based on data published or generated elsewhere (Eichner, 1983, p. x). Their authors remain 'like physiologists who have never dissected; like astronomers who have never seen the stars' (Bagehot, 1880, p. 7).

Leontief continues:

> Nothing reveals the aversion of the great majority of present-day academic economists for systematic empirical inquiry more than the methodological devices that they employ to avoid or cut short the use of concrete factual information. Instead of constructing theoretical models capable of preserving the identity of hundreds, even thousands, of variables needed for the concrete description and analysis of a modern economy, they first of all resort to 'aggregation'. The primary information, however detailed, is packaged in a relatively small system of equations describing the entire economy in terms of a small number of corresponding 'aggregative' variables. The fitting, as a rule, is accomplished by means of 'least squares' or another similar curve-fitting procedure. (Eichner, 1983, p. viii)

The findings of this procedure are likely to be *ipso facto* tautological or false. Thomas Balogh went even further, arguing that it 'has produced a body of theory which is at worst positively misleading and at best merely vacuous' (Whynes, 1984, p. 162).

Fifty years ago the young Friedrich Hayek also issued a warning against attempts to establish causal relations between aggregates or general averages: 'it will never be possible to establish necessary connections of cause and effect between them as we can between individual phenomena, individual price, etc. I would even go so far as to assert that, from the very nature of economic theory, averages can never form a link in its reasoning' (Hayek, 1935, pp. 4–5).

The Phillips Curve is a good illustration of the errors arising from aggregation: a different meaning must be attached to a lot of unemployment in a few industries or a little unemployment in a lot of industries, even though the weighted average is identical, and ditto for wage rate changes. When you correlate two statistical series thus composed, the possibilities of error are squared.

'There is perhaps no manner of reasoning that exposes itself to more errors than that which consists of constructing a hypothetical world entirely different from the real world, for the purpose of applying one's calculations' (Sismondi, 1827, p. 329). It is from what are euphemistically called 'simplifying assumptions' that these economic imaginings are derived. The model-builder is by convention allowed to include any assumptions he likes. There is even a certain prestige attached to those that are outstandingly absurd. Thereafter, the idea is that assumptions should be progressively unsimplified until reality is regained. 'But for the most part this "optimistic" procedure just has not worked out at all fruitfully, and, as regards our fundamental assumptions about knowledge, expectations and certainty, it seems that *it simply cannot work out*' (Terence Hutchison in Wiles and Routh, 1984, p. 5).

Some theorists have the grace to admit that their models are remote from practical significance. Professor Malinvaud, having presented his model complete with the usual fantasies, explains that the econometrics of investment is still far from being able to handle its applications. Economists in the past thirty years have been thinking within a framework of frictionless general equilibrium. 'Profitability, which is a disequilibrium concept, had no role to play in such a framework and was therefore overlooked' (Malvinvaud, 1982, pp. 11–12). Nickell, too, recognises the limitations of his econometric demonstrations: 'Although we have identified a number of possible important factors in this macro time series context, unless we obtain micro-economic confirmation of these results they will remain as little more than tentative conjectures' (Nickell, September 1982, p. 571).

More usually, though, theorists follow the example of their revered ancestor, Léon Walras, who claimed that his pure theory of economics resembled the physico-mathematical sciences in every respect. It abstracted and defined ideal-type concepts, constructed *a priori* the whole framework of theorems and proofs, and then went back to experience not to confirm but to apply the conclusions (Walras, 1874, p. 71).

With these considerations in mind, let us critically examine the stalking horses with which their users claim to have captured the secrets of the economy. We have made their acquaintance in Chapter 4, but the time has now come to bring them to judgment.

5.2   SUPPLY-SIDE ECONOMICS

'Supply creates its own demand' Say asserted to those who remarked that a shortage of demand had caused a 'general glut'. Say's ideas have been revived in the doctrines of supply-side economics. For example, Mr Nigel Lawson, Chancellor of the Exchequer, in an article in *The Sunday Times*, 30 December 1984, p. 16: 'the shortcomings of the British Economy lie not with a failure of demand, but with a failure of supply'. The term carries a suggestion of national development corporations busily encouraging old enterprises and promoting new ones, but this is not its intent. Instead, it has to do with marginal tax rates: if we relieve the rich of some of their tax burden they will be encouraged to work harder and earn more, so that production, savings and investment will rise. Mr Reagan and Mrs Thatcher did this immediately they came to power. Indeed, the curve invented by Arthur Laffer, relating tax rate to tax yield, purports to demonstrate that a reduction in marginal tax rates would stimulate such a rise in income that the total tax yield will be maintained. Complementary policies concern the reduction of government expenditure (much of which aids the poor at the expense of the not-so-poor) and the subsitution of expenditure tax for income tax. In a memorandum to the US Secretary of the Treasury (November 1974), Laffer explained, 'Taxes of all sorts must be reduced. These reductions will be most effective where they lower *marginal* tax rates most. Any reduction in marginal rates means that the employer will pay less and yet the employees will receive more. Both from the employer and employee point of view *more employment will be desired and more output will be forthcoming*' (Rousseas, 1981, p. 197). It is true that, as inflation rose, successive Chancellors have gone lower and lower in the pay hierarchy to collect income tax (see Brittan; above, p. 89, so that it is high time the tax threshold should be raised. But in Britain and the United States it is the highest income earners who have been most benefited. Non-progressive expenditure taxes have been substituted for progressive income taxes, while cuts are made in public expenditure and funds raised by the sale of public assets.

5.3   SEARCH UNEMPLOYMENT

No less surprising is the doctrine of *search unemployment* expounded in Chapter 4. For orthodox economists, involuntary unemployment was always a distasteful notion, for it meant that the labour market did not clear, as all respectable markets were supposed to do. They substituted an idea more to their liking: encouraged by governments and trade unions, people got 'choosy' about the jobs they were prepared to accept, so that market-clearing was impeded. Professor Lucas of Chicago was quoted to the effect that unemployment was bad luck and to that extent involuntary, but that all unemployment was voluntary to the extent that 'however miserable one's current work options, one can always choose to accept them' (Lucas, 1981, p. 242).

Guy Standing identifies seven elements whereby involuntary unemployment has been assumed away: **Inactive unemployment** deemed to apply to those of the recorded unemployed who do not actively search for jobs and who, it is argued, cannot therefore want work very much and, by implication, do not need it very much. But is it really reasonable to expect workers to search for jobs known to be unavailable? 'Indeed, someone looking for something that does not exist could legitimately be regarded as irrational and thus deserving to be excluded from a count of the available unemployed' (Standing, 1981, pp. 564–5). Then there are those with **unrealistic job aspirations** who seek jobs for which they are not qualified; those with **excessive wage aspirations**; those with **casual or short-time work preferences**; those who have '**voluntarily quit**' their jobs; '**marginal' workers** – casual or 'secondary' workers with weak labour force attachment; those who are dissuaded from accepting jobs by **unemployment insurance and other transfer mechanisms**.

He summarises, 'The distinction between voluntary and involuntary unemployment is essentially a rhetorical one, with ideological overtones. Because any definition of voluntary unemployment must be somewhat arbitrary, the claims that it is widespread are very difficult to refute. But equally such claims, with all their implicit assumptions, are extremely hard to support empirically' (Standing, 1981, p. 576). And on the theory behind the claims: 'This so-called neo-classical model effectively defined all unemployed as voluntary, to the extent that "jobseeking" itself became a job. The approach crystallised in an influential volume edited by Edmund Phelps, who stated categorically. "Today's unemployment is an investment in a better allocation . . . of employed persons tomorrow"' (ibid. p. 564).

Peter Wiles explains the intellectual process involved. 'Is unemployment a little large to seem voluntary? – let us invent "search", and have the proletariat *cyclically* decide to give up their wages in order to spend their days looking for betterment opportunities they know aren't there' (Wiles and Routh, 1984, p. 306).

5.4 RATIONAL EXPECTATIONS

Is the theory of rational expectations any more promising? It was devised to remedy a flaw in the notion of perfect competition and general equilibrium: decision-makers required perfect foresight in order to optimise the effects of their decisions, failing which, they might go horribly and unpredictably wrong.

But *nil desperandum*! Let us follow the advice given by Hamlet to his mother: assume a virtue if you have it not. In this case, the virtue is *rational expectations*. These are the expectations you would entertain if you had a grasp of orthodox economics and a supply of the appropriate statistical tables. The Liverpool Model used by Professor Minford includes a term for rational expectations, meaning thereby that the decision-makers believe what the Liverpool model forecasts. Note that two separate assumptions are employed: one, that it is possible to predict the future by applying principles of maximisation, and, two, that this is what entrepreneurs, workers and other decision-makers actually do. Given these, the theorists 'know' that rewards will be maximised and, by process of marginal adjustment, the market will clear. We are the lucky inhabitants of a capitalist Utopia, ignorant and ungrateful though we may be.

Over the years, there has been much criticism of the misleading nature of this and related economic doctrines. No one had been able to catch a business actually engaged in the process of marginal adjustment, equating marginal costs with marginal revenue, with unit costs falling with falling output and vice versa. Indeed, businessmen (unless they were economics graduates) did not know what economists were talking about when they questioned them along these lines. The result was that orthodox economists refrained from questioning them. Economists who thought it important and continued to do so came up with answers that were quite different from those suggested by the textbooks. If industrialists had sat for economics exams they would have failed. (For reports on and interpretations of empirical studies see Andrews, 1949; Andrews and Wilson, 1951; and for a modern statement, Dennis Mueller, Hiroyuki Odagiri, Peter Wiles and Frederic Lee in Wiles and Routh, 1984.)

In *Positive Economics* (1953) Friedman boldly dismissed complaints against the accepted theory. It is of no consequence why businessmen think they do what they do as long as what they do has the consequences that would follow if they did what we (the economists) say that they do. I am, of course, paraphrasing his views. C. E. Ferguson and J. P. Gould expound them with eminent clarity: 'For the purpose of *explaining* business behaviour it is sufficient to assume that entrepreneurs act *as if* they tried to maximize profit. For the purpose of predicting business behaviour the *as if* assumption is the only justifiable one' (Ferguson and Gould, 1975, p. 221. Quoted in Katouzian, 1980, p. 82).

But apart from the correctness or otherwise of predictions, may not the unreality of assumptions itself be a source of error? This suggestion, Friedman audaciously replies, 'is fundamentally wrong and productive of much mischief'. It is a positive advantage for assumptions to be unrealistic: 'to be important . . . a hypothesis must be descriptively false in its assumptions' (Friedman, 1953, p. 14. Quoted in Blaug, 1980, p. 105).

So the decision-makers behave *as if* they entertained rational expectations (as defined) and therefore their behaviour is maximising and optimising. But how do we know that the outcome of business activities coincides with what would happen if businessmen and others behaved according to the neo-classical code? The short answer is, we do not. We know they do not follow the code and, in truth, we have no idea what would happen if they did. It is, indeed, probable that the whole economy would collapse.

You may have noticed the references to 'shocks' and 'surprises' in Chapter 4, and perhaps you will now see their significance. How come rational expectations do not lead to the neo-classical promised land? It is because the rational expectations must have been disappointed because of shocks and surprises. Decisions have gone wrong because the participants guessed wrong. This leads to the proposition that government policies will fail to influence events unless they are sprung on the world as a surprise. If the players have forseen them, they will have taken evasive action.

I have of necessity dealt briefly with these interesting doctrines. For more extensive treatments, see Blaug (1980, ch. 4), and Katouzian (1980, ch. 3).

5.5   THE NATURAL RATE OF UNEMPLOYMENT

The natural rate of unemployment is an appendage of rational expectations. The term suggests something inevitable, even benign, against which resistance would be useless. In Chapter 4 we met a variety of definitions: it is that rate of unemployment that conforms with anticipations and maintains a constant rate of inflation; surprises cause temporary deviations, but in due course employment returns to a level determined by real factors; these are 'the effectiveness of the labor market, the extent of competition or monopoly, the barriers or encouragements to working in various occupations, and so on' (Friedman, 1977, p. 458); it is that *hypothetical* unemployment percentage which *would be* observed in any period if the number of jobs on offer were equal to the number of persons wishing to hold jobs; it is determined by such factors as the costs of gathering information about job vacancies in a given market; it is that level of unemployment that would suffice to stop inflation accelerating; it is that level of unemployment at which wage rates would rise as fast as labour productivity when inflation is zero; it is the Non-accelerating Inflation Rate of Unemployment (NAIRU).

Miller and Wood propose that the Department of Employment should be required to publish annual estimates of the natural rate of unemployment. I suggest that it is immeasurable, a figment of the imagination of people who want to take unemployment out of politics by persuading us that it is part of the natural order of things.

5.6   INSTITUTIONAL ENGINEERING

The theories discussed above are the creations of economists who, like Archbishop Whately and Stanley Jevons, believe in the magic of the market. The two sections that follow are of a different order for they incorporate the views of people who see the economy not as a system of self-regulating mechanical forces, but of interacting institutions regulated by the behaviour of people who themselves are subject to social influences. The problem then becomes how to socialise behaviour in such a way as to moderate the destructive effects of the self-seeking postulated by neo-classical theories.

5.6.1   Trade Unions and Unemployment

Section 2.3 of Chapter 4 asked 'Do trade unions cause unemployment?' Readers seeking an unambiguous reply to that question will have been disappointed, for some of the theorists answer a categorical 'Yes', and others an emphatic 'No'.

If you believe that competitive markets set prices for goods and services at that level where the amounts offered for sale (at that price) equal the amounts sought for purchase (at the same price), then, with Patrick Minford, you will say 'Yes', for unions set the prices for their members' labour above the free competitive level and thus reduce the amount demanded. But, even if this were so, Samuel Brittan replies, while monopolies cause the price of their product to be higher than non-monopolies, they do not cause a continuing relative rise. This view is supported by other theorists who agree that unionisation causes a once-for-all rise, with a more or less permanent differential over the non-unionised.

This is not an entirely logical deduction, for trade unions, at each set of negotiations, endeavour to push up rates beyond what would prevail without their intervention. After each set of negotiations, demand for the labour of their members would be reduced and the gap between the unionised and non-unionised sector further widened. But the statistics show that this does not in fact happen, so the theorists have to content themselves by postulating a once-for-all differential. But the extent of differential is unfortunately incalculable, for when wage changes in a unionised industry are compared with those in a non-unionised one it is on the assumption of other-things-being-equal, which they never are. It also depends on an absence of feedback between industries, and feedback is a well-documented phenomenon (see, for instance, Wragg and Robertson, 1976). The high-level of guesswork in such estimates is demonstrated by the wide differences between them.

In the neo-classical model, the response of an employer to a rise in labour costs is to dismiss some of his workers. He cannot pass on the additional costs in higher prices because the price is dictated by the market, but he can reduce his marginal costs (the cost of producing the last unit of output) by dismissing some workers and reducing output. Thus he will continue to maximise profit (or, be it noted, minimise losses).

Paradoxically, employers in the real world have a number of options, but this is not one of them: they cannot cut unit costs by producing less. The further output falls below full capacity, the higher do unit costs become. Since, by contrast, they normally operate below capacity, they can compensate for the rise in labour costs by raising output and enjoying the economies of scale. They would then have to allocate more of their resources to the effort of selling. They may also increase the selling price of their products and often do. Indeed, in a prolonged period of inflation such as we are now experiencing, periodical price rises are taken for granted. Firms can also try to work more efficiently: it is not unusual to combine a pay increase with an efficiency drive or to include a reduction of restrictive practices as part of the bargain.

Managers are not helpless victims of circumstances over which they have no control, sliding up and down the textbook curves like passengers on a switchback railway. Survival demands the exercise of many strategies about which a flourishing literature has been established. The existence of a unionised workforce may help or hinder this process.

It is true that in countries with a regimented labour force business has flourished: Taiwan, Singapore, Hong Kong, Thailand and, until recently, South Korea and South Africa. In these cases, the cost has been long hours, low pay and the loss of security and human dignity.

But do trade unions, through their success at raising pay, accelerate the substitution of capital for labour? My observations suggest that mechanisation and automation commend themselves to managers because they substitute obedient and predictable machines for fractious and capricious human beings, whether or not the latter are organised. In the textbooks we are shown nice smooth isoquants along which capital can be substituted for labour and vice versa, but in the untidy world the substitution of one technique for another requires a quantum jump that does not lend itself to marginal analysis. Empirical investigation cannot be avoided if it is desired to discover when and how it will happen and what the consequences are likely to be.

5.6.2 Incomes Policies

Trade unions may, however, cause unemployment by a less direct means. They promote the rise of money wages in ways unconnected with increases in productivity (see Wragg and Robertson, 1976). The rise in wage-costs does not squeeze profits but is passed on in higher prices, with profit margins sustained in percentage terms. Imports are encouraged from countries enjoying a lower rise in costs, exports suffer, balance of payments difficulties ensue, and governments are thus persuaded to introduce deflationary measures. Interest rates are raised thus placing a handicap on firms that want to borrow for purposes of trade or investment; banks may be required to deposit additional amounts with the central bank, thus causing them to curb lending to businessmen and the public; public expenditure is reduced and thus incomes and employment; taxes on expenditure may be raised, forming an additional tax on employment; public corporations may be privatised thus diverting savings from looking for new investment. High interest rates attract funds from abroad, so that, temporarily, the balance of payments becomes more favourable. In the longer term, interest must be paid on these funds, raising the cost of the public debt and, in so far they are foreign-owned, worsening the balance of payments. These government-imposed penalties for cost-inflation may be seen in action today in the United States, United Kingdom, France and the German Federal Republic.

In most countries governments have also experimented with incomes policies which, if they had succeeded, would have made these other measures unnecessary. Belief in the possible benefits of incomes policies presupposes a belief that social institutions play an important role in the making of economic decisions, and that these institutions can be influenced by law or by persuasion and agreement. It also suggests an acceptance of Keynesian remedies, for such policies would restrain inflation in times of prosperity, and enable governments to prime economies to avert depression. Monetarists, by contrast, assert that with sound monetary management, incomes policies are unnecessary; without it, useless.

Deflationary measures present a bonanza to money-lenders; to the rest of humanity they are a misery worth while making an effort to avoid. Then why do employers, trade unions and their members not unite to operate anti-inflationary agreements? Metcalf, Layard and Meade, as we saw in 4.2.4 above, believe that the benefits of a pay policy would be so great that they could and should be achieved by the exercise of compulsion. But the record of past policies is discouraging. They have been most effective in the short periods of wage-freeze or zero-norm, but these short periods are followed by feverish activity to make up for lost ground that may possibly take pay rates to higher levels than they would otherwise have reached.

Econometricians have attempted to measure the effect of incomes policies in Britain and the United States by comparing periods without policies with those when policies were in force. Some claim that such policies have had a perverse effect. 'The main conclusion, demonstrated by consideration of a variety of models, is that the policy-off period was far from a homogenous interlude; it follows that the comparison of policy-on and policy-off periods is a dangerous procedure, in that the policy-off results do not provide a sufficiently firm foundation for predicting what would have happened in the absence of incomes policy' (Michael T. Sumner in Parkin and Sumner, 1972, p. 179).

There are not many people who believe that pay controls can be enforced by law or taxation: as Phelps Brown remarked (p. 95 above), this is administratively impracticable. Thus pay restraints require considerable voluntary support from those who are to be required to exercise them. But, in contrast to the era of the medieval Just Wage, there is no agreement about who ought to get what. Even in Sweden, with centralised pay bargaining between the employers' and trade union federations, Professor T. L. Johnston reports, 'The efforts to find some kind of comprehensive job description system for the economy and an agreed set of job evaluation criteria have . . . been half-hearted, and have now been largely abandoned, in favour of the crude horsetrading in the course of pay rounds' (Owen Smith, 1981, p. 113).

Yet, on an overall view, the results of the system of pay bargaining have been ludicrous. The Department of Employment annual New Earnings Survey registers an increase in average earnings (for male and female employees aged 18 and over) of 88 per cent between April 1978 and April 1983. But real gross domestic product between 1978 and the second quarter of 1983 had increased by just over 2 per cent. Inflation was powerfully at work, with most of the increased pay swallowed up by a rise in retail prices of 71 per cent. Yet these arithmetic changes were won at the cost of great effort in research and the preparation of memoranda, many hours of negotiation, much arbitration and 25 million working days lost in strikes (*Employment Gazette*, November 1984, pp. S7, S44 and S50). Not all the strikes were concerned with pay, yet enormous energy was burnt up, not so much for an improvement in living standards, but by everyone desperately trying to keep up with or ahead of everyone else.

It is difficult for those without experience of industrial relations, as practitioners or close observers, to understand the complexity and uncertainty with which pay changes are determined, something exacerbated by the decentralisation of the process since the 1950s, and the collapse of the traditional conceptions of what was fair and reasonable. For studies of the subject, see W. W. Daniel in Blackaby, 1980, Chapter 7, and G. A. Walker reported in Routh, 1980, pp. 210–11.

'It cannot be expected, in a context of distributional dissent, that trade unions will exercise restraint in pay bargaining as in effect an act of simple altruism towards the rest of the community.' (Crouch and Pizzorno, 1978, p. 35). Pay determination is an integral part of the competitive process that is supposed to be the *modus vivendi* of market economies. 'it is also apparent that unionism is essentialy *a product of* liberal capitalism and, as it presently exists, is dependent upon this form of capitalism for its very *raison d'etre*' (ibid. p. 42).

6 Options, Strategies and Prognoses

6.1 DISILLUSION

The theories we have examined have been at best over-simplifications, at worst products of 'bad conscience and the evil intent of apologetic'. They were conceived in isolation from the world, developed *in vacuo* and, when applied by governments, had effects disconcertingly different from those anticipated.

Keynes warned of the complications that might follow the application of his expansionary measures. 'With the confused psychology which often prevails, the Government programme may, through its effect on "confidence" . . . retard other investment unless measures are taken to offset it' (Keynes, 1936, p. 120). The perverse reactions to government measures have been evident in Labour-governed Britain and in President Mitterrand's France. Yet so capricious are the controllers of wealth that their funds are mustered to the support of the US dollar when the Reagan administration breaks all bounds in its borrowing requirement and the deficit in its balance of trade. Every monetarist rule is broken: employment and output rise, inflation falls.

My thesis has been that capitalism's tendency to periodic mass unemployment is inherent in its decision-making process. Feedback, as we have seen, augments the operative forces so that 'unreasonable hopes and unreasonable fears alternately rule with tyrannical sway' (Mill, above, p. 61). The great paradox of the competitive system is that unreasonable hopes and fears become reasonable as soon as enough people share them.

Governments show a diminishing power to control this process, even when their judgement is not impaired by arcane economic dogmas, for it is not governments but the giant corporations that ordain the international deployment of resources. Industrialists call on governments to protect their overseas investments, and bankers

114

expect them to bail them out when the debts of foreign governments are not repaid, but, for themselves, they distribute their investments about the world to suit their own convenience. While governments wrestle with problems of international co-operation, jealously guarding their own sovereignty, the giant corporations have surmounted national frontiers, thus escaping government control. Is Japanese competition unbeatable? Then embark on joint ventures with the Japanese. Is a national industry stricken with structural decay? Then extend your investments in the country that is threatening it. Not to do so would be a dereliction of duty to your shareholders and to your team of managers.

6.2 PALLIATIVES

If unemployment (cyclical, structural and regional) is a built-in characteristic of capitalism, a psychologically-determined effect of atomised decision-making, then we must either learn to live with it or change the system. But its effects can be mitigated, like those of an incurable disease, just as they can be exacerbated by wrong or ill-intentioned policies.

It would be helpful if governments better understood the nature and evolution of unemployment and its connection with inflation. As G. D. N. Worswick told the Bank of England, 'Policy in Britain today appears to be based on the belief that once inflation has been brought down, and held down for a while, it will be exorcised for ever. The hard lessons of unemployment will be learned once for all. We may do well to remember that after 1926 British trade unions were unusually weak, and the climate of stable or even falling prices became firmly established. Even so, money wages stopped falling in 1934, when unemployment was still 17 per cent and they were rising at 3 per cent per annum in 1937 and 1938 when unemployment was still around 11 per cent' (Worswick, 1984, p. 25).

The trade cycle is operating on a world scale, affecting even socialist countries because of the fall in demand for their exports, but in due course and without much warning, pessimism will be replaced by optimism as the cycle turns. Self-fulfilling hopes will predominate and, for a while, we shall never have had it so good again. Government policies are delaying this change but they cannot prevent it. An expansionary policy would speed the process: lowering of interest rates, the contraction of the public sector put into reverse, expansion in education, scientific research, housing and the health service. Industrialists have been urging such changes, but Derek Aldcroft warns that financial interests would do their best to frustrate policies for reflation. 'And past experience in both Britain and France suggests that they have sufficient power to be able to do just that' (Aldcroft, 1984, p. 158). For their success, expansionary policies would require much more international co-ordination than they have received in the past, for a government in isolation is an easy prey for those who oppose them.

6.3   EVOLUTION AND ADAPTATION

Capitalist systems vary from country to country and change over time. Is it possible that they may rid themselves of their defects by their own development? Since the second World War much thought and effort has gone into the avoidance or reduction of conflict, in the belief that this would result in more stable and prosperous societies. Concensus, pluralism, co-determination and corporatism are all modes of thought concerned with such possibilities.

The co-determination provisions in West German law were designed to promote these ideals, but their achievements have been disappointing (Owen Smith, 1981, pp. 183–5; Gourevitch, 1984, pp. 94–102).

In Britain important changes have been brought about by the Redundancy Payments Act of 1965 and the Industrial Relations Act of 1971 and its successors. But the most ambitious project in this respect has been lost in the sands of time. The Committee of Inquiry on Industrial Democracy (the Bullock Committee) was appointed by a Labour government in 1975. But in Britain, as in Germany, there was no meeting of minds between the trade union and employers' confederations (Marsden, 1978, p. 56). In 1977 the Committee's report recommended wide-ranging innovations but there was no clamourous campaign in their support. Six years later, Charles Hanson and Paul Rathkey held a survey of workers' opinions. 'It is clear from this survey that shopfloor workers do want more say in workplace decision-making, particularly in task-related areas and matters of manpower planning and work organisation. However, they generally place limits on the extent of that involvement. The desire for more say falls far short of joint decision-making. While board representation is desired . . . the cause of workers' control attracts little sympathy' (Hanson and Rathkey, 1984, p. 166).

The Swedes, like the British, have felt the need to convert custom and practice into law, and did so in a series of acts in the 1970s. But progress in workplace participation agreements has been disappointing (Johnston, 1981, pp. 116–18; Gourevitch, 1984, p. 328).

Unions in Europe have long been concerned with their failure to achieve a more equitable distribution in the ownership of wealth. If pay agreements included a provision for contributions to investment funds, perhaps they might be able to buy their way into positions of greater power? The employer might make contributions to a savings fund administered by the appropriate union or might pay by the transfer of shares in the company so that, one day, the workers might become majority share-holders. Even a small holding would afford some influence in extracting information and in persuading the company to extend its investments in socially acceptable ways rather than, for example, real estate in the United States. German trade unions already own two of the top 100 companies in Germany (Owen Smith, 1983, p. 207). Scandinavian unions are also seeking to move in this direction, the Swedes through the Meidner Plan (see Meidner, 1978, and Gourevitch, 1984, pp. 272–5).

But though the Swedish LO (the manual union federation) adopted the Meidner Plan just before the 1976 parliamentary election, the Social Democratic Party fought shy of endorsing it. They lost the election. As the 1982 election approached a campaign was launched against the plan, that the Social Democrats had now adopted. Wage-earner investment funds were denounced 'as a grave threat to Swedish democracy as well as the economy by the bourgeios parties and organized business. . . . An amount of money unprecedented in Swedish politics was poured into an apparent effort to make the election turn on the issue, which was defined as a matter of saving Sweden from being transformed into an East European dictatorship. . . . The massive campaign against the funds did not prevent the Social Democrats from returning to office' (Gourevitch, 1984, p. 328).

The Danes follow the German pattern, with employees electing a third of the members of their company's supervisory board, but on joint ownership they have been no more successful than the Swedes: a draft law on this subject was defeated when it was presented to parliament in 1982 (European Communities, 1982, p. 5).

The Nordic model for employee investment funds commends itself because it seems to be a painless way of transforming society. To Marxists, 'Industrial relations are equated with a power struggle which is itself based on an irreconcilable contradiction between capital-owners and wage-workers. Durable regulation, i.e. a stable relationship pattern between capital and labour, is impossible since the industrial conflict itself is unresolvable' (Schienstock, 1981, p. 185). But the Meidner scheme would enable labour to acquire capital not by confiscation but by buying shares through ordinary financial institutions. As Hans-Göran Myrdal puts it, 'it could be made to seem consistent with the reformist traditions of Swedish social democracy'. But this, as we have noted, is not at all how it was viewed from the right. '. . . what should be stated is that the scheme is revolutionary at least as far as its consequences are concerned. It would completely change Swedish society, the labour market and industrial relations. The Meidner scheme and the ideas it represents are the main threat to the Swedish model' (Myrdal, 1980, p. 59).

6.4   MUTUAL ACCOMMODATION

While 19th century socialists alarmed the bourgeoisie by predicting the imminent end of capitalism, there was no shortage of writers who reassured them by portraying it as a system that was benign, even ideal, in whose preservation the interests of all classes converged. This was the basis of the *consensus* politics vigorously promoted in the 1950s and 60s, but which is first encountered in Monchrétien's text of 1615, where the classes complement one another in a divinely-designed *entelechie* of States (Routh, 1975, p. 32). 'Pluralism' constituted a less sanguine doctrine: class conflict existed, but none the less the parties could agree to differ. Objectives and choice of solutions might diverge, but the conflict is not unresolvable: 'the ideological premise of this approach is rather a philosophy of mutual survival' (Schienstock, 1981, p. 174). More recently 'neo-corporatism' has held sway, with its suggestions of permanent corporations of employers, trade unions and governments, their struggles constrained by mutual accommodation (see Streeck, 1981).

Marx invisaged that, through their organisations, employed and unemployed workers would co-operate to weaken the despotism of capital, exercised by the law of supply and demand (Marx, 1887, p. 640). But the deprivation inflicted on the proletariat has been only relative, as, indeed, Marx observed: 'although the comforts of the labourer have risen, the social satisfaction which they give has fallen in comparison with these augmented comforts of the capitalist. . . . Our wants and their satisfaction have their origin in society.' (Freedman, 1961, p. 63). Output per head of population showed something like a fourfold increase in the 19th century, while consumers' expenditure at constant prices more than doubled between 1900 and 1965 (Routh, 1984, p. 40). Between 1965 and 1984, real average employee earnings rose by 33 per cent.

Until 1911, the unemployed had to rely for relief on the Poor Law, unless they were members of a trade union insurance fund, but in that year the National Insurance Act was passed. In return for the payment of 5 (old) pence a week (split between the worker and his employer) an unemployed worker was entitled to 7 shillings a week up to a maximum of 15 weeks in a year (Beveridge, 1930, pp. 263–7). To convert these prices into the pounds and (new) pence of 1984, one must mutliply by a factor of about 30. Thus the worker's contribution of 1911 would equal 62½ pence, and the weekly benefit would be £10.50.

In 1930, deductions for adult men were 7 (old) pence a week, and the employer's contribution 8 pence. Benefit for an adult man was 17 shillings a week, with 9 shillings for his wife or other adult dependant and 2 shillings for each dependent child. In January 1984 values: £1.16 in contributions (employer's and employee's combined), with £15.78 benefit for an adult man, £8.35 for his wife and £1.80 for each child.

The man of 1930 paid the equivalent of 54p a week (in 1984 prices), the man of 1984, £10.38. Unemployment pay for the man and wife of 1930 (in 1984 prices) would have been £24.13, and the man and his wife of 1984, £43.75. Real contributions have increased by a factor of 19, and benefit by a factor of 1.8. Relative to wage rates, unemployment pay is half what it was, while contributions are five times as great (sources: Routh, 1980,pp. 134–5; *Employment Gazette*, Feb. 1984, Tables 5.8 and 6.4; Beveridge, 1930, pp. 277–8).

6.5 STALEMATE OR RADICAL CHANGE

As long as real incomes continue to rise, with unemployment pay rising too (though not so fast), will the electorate ever demonstrate its readiness for radical change? There may be no practical answer to the question 'What is to be done?' so that we and our children are condemned to an infinite series of booms and slumps, while 'wealth accumulates, and men decay'. Oliver Goldsmith made his comment two centuries ago, and the process still continues.

In the past, wars have functioned to achieve and, for a time, maintain full employment, with the reserve army of the unemployed conscripted into uniform or industry. Can it be done without their occurrence? Derek H. Aldcroft is pessimistic. 'After a prolonged period of mass unemployment it is clearly very difficult to get back to full employment quickly. The sheer magnitude of the problem – some 3 million unemployed in the 1930s and again at present – means that a very rapid rate of expansion of the economy would be required to re-absorb these numbers back into the active labour force at a time when the latter itself is still expanding. Against this background there would appear to be little prospect that spontaneous economic recovery could solve the problem. An element of recovery will undoubtedly follow the current recession but it is unlikely to be sufficient to break the back of the unemployment problem. The strong natural boom of the 1930s took time to dent the unemployment total and even at the peak there was still a residue of nearly 1½ million out of work' (Aldcroft, 1984, p. 157).

The trouble is that market economies do not lend themselves at all well to government-inspired expansion because of what Keynes called the 'confused psychology' that often prevails (see above, p. 114). Business sentiment is highly infectious. More particularly, those with money to deploy are extremely shy: like the antelope of the Serengeti plain, they panic first and ask questions afterwards. This is a code for survival. With the financiers, there are even financial prizes for those that lead the stampede, and forfeits for those that lag.

The Meidner Plan evoked an hysterical response from the wealth-owners of Sweden, and there is some substance in the assessment of Glynn and Harrison of the probable effect of the Labour Party's Alternative Economic Strategy: 'With the government issuing directives, appointing official trustees and nationalising firms which refused to fall into line, capital's priority would be to defend its control over production. . . . It would cease investment, cut back on production, refuse to release essential stocks, ship assets abroad and whatever else it deemed necessary. The result would be economic and social chaos' (above, p. 101). What Berle and Means observed fifty years ago applies *a fortiori* today: 'The rise of the modern corporation has brought a concentration of economic power which can compete on equal terms with the modern state. . . . The state seeks in some aspects to regulate the corporation, while the corporation, steadily becoming more powerful, makes every effort to avoid such regulation. Where its own interests are concerned it even attempts to dominate the state' (Berle and Means, 1935, p. 357).

6.6 HISTORICAL IMPERATIVES

Britain is sensitive to external events because it is heavily dependent on international trade. But there is another compelling reason for international involvement with direct relevance to the need to create jobs. There were about 2000 million people in the world in 1930, 3000 million in 1960 and 4500 million in 1981. 'The Bureau of Statistics of the ILO has published information which links these trends to the employment question. The population in the 15 to 24 age group in the developed countries increased from 144 million in 1960 to 192 million in 1980 but is projected to fall to 176 million by the end of the present decade. In contrast, in the developing countries the population in this age group increased from 371 million in 1960 to 665 million in 1980 and is expected to reach 893 million by the year 2000. This means that these countries will have to create some 230 million additional jobs in the period from 1980 to 2000 to maintain the 1980 rate of employment' (International Institute for Labour Studies, 1984, p. 13).

The response to the Ethiopian famine has demonstrated that amongst the British electorate there is a strong desire to assist people in need. That is one good reason why the British should help in the creation of the additional jobs needed in the Third World. Another is the threat to world stability of a massive rise in destitution. But to help others create jobs we shall have to improve our will to help ourselves.

It is an understandable feature of economic development that, with it, people show a diminishing willingness to undertake dirty, arduous and boring jobs. In many advanced industrial countries this is partly met by the import of workers from poorer places. But it also encourages the migration of industry to countries with masses of people eager to get industrial jobs. Third World countries see this corporate invasion as a threat to their independence, but, as Joan Robinson used to say, 'There is only one thing worse than being exploited by a multinational corporation – and that is not being exploited by a multinational corporation'.

Reducing unemployment is made more difficult because we are assailed on two fronts: there is the cyclical phenomenon that is endemic in a system of atomised decision-making; and there is that aspect of competition in which the industry of one country is attacked by that of another, so that a nation may find parts of its productive system in decay. International depression could be reduced if all countries concerned co-ordinated their policies, reduced (instead of raising) interest rates, presented a united (and thus impregnable) defence against financial speculation and promoted public or private investment in accordance with the availability of resources. In the past, attempts to do this have failed because it entails drastic restrictions on national sovereignty and in the relative power of corporations and governments. No country could achieve these ends on its own without a drastic change of social and political system.

Defence on the second front requires every country to find and fill a place in the world that will allow people to earn their living with dignity, relieved from the misery of unemployment and the drudgery of unrewarding toil. World development cannot proceed without developed countries losing industries to those that are less developed. They cannot deny the right of the less developed to learn, take over and outdo them in certain respects. It is for the trade union internationals and the International Labour Office to see that the transplanted industries benefit the workers in the countries to which they are transferred, and do not increase their misery.

This is a compelling reason why countries like Britain must develop their scientific and cultural resources. We have lagged behind the Scandinavians in primary and secondary education and behind the Swiss and Germans in technical education, and Mrs Thatcher's government has been dismantling what was our exemplary university system. The bulk of our population remains semi-literate and semi-numerate: yet we have the resources to educate them properly and to act as a leading centre for higher education for the rest of the world. Our educational services are an asset that can be developed without cost to the balance of payments; they are in fact an invisible export of great potential. Instead of making teachers redundant we should be raising their level of education, and thus that of those they are supposed to educate.

According to the population census of 1981, scientists and mathematicians (employed as such) constituted 0.44 per cent of the occupied population of Great Britain. Electronic engineers formed 0.15 per cent. And yet, according to a survey by the Japanese Ministry of International Trade and Industry, of the world's 'significant' inventions since the Second World War, Britain has produced 55 per cent, the United States 22 per cent and Japan 6 per cent (Roger Eglin,

Sunday Times Business News, 20 January 1985, p. 53). The British environment has been favourable to invention; it should not be beyond our wit to keep it so.

Indeed, in the years ahead the inhabitants of the United Kingdom are going to have to live off their wits, preferably not in the financial sweat-shops, glimpsed in television news, in which stock and foreign-exchange brokers ply their frenetic trade, but in the pursuit of scientific discovery and in the design and construction of the electronic devices that will take over the physical work of production. Just as in ancient Athens the Athenians were released by their slaves to follow pursuits of art and culture, so will our robots free us for more enthralling activities that will fill the hours now spent in mines, factories, shops and offices.

It does not make sense to panic at the prospect, as if we were going to run out of useful and rewarding things to do. There is no shortage of talents; all we need is to employ our resources in their cultivation. Britain can be a centre for world education and research, for health services and the arts. We are still ahead in some of these spheres, and by the time the rest of the world catches up with our present position, we can be as far ahead again.

I am sketching these possibilities because it is essential that they do not get lost in the noise of the day-to-day world. They are matters of public choice, for whose achievement concerted effort will be required. The constraints are political, not economic; questions not of resources but of will. As John Goldthorpe has said, 'the attempt made to change the boundaries of the political in relation to the economy must at the same time be seen as an attempt to shift the actual balance of power and advantage in society; and the achievement of such a shift would be as integral to the success of the policies pursued as the movement of economic variables in the direction desired' (Goldthorpe, 1983, p. 82). In Chapters 4 and 5, above, we have encountered the works of the monetarists and the neo-neo-classicists who promote 'the new laissez-faire' and whose policies clash with those of the post-Keynesians, social democrats and Marxists. Goldthorpe translates the conflict from economics to politics: 'what would be entailed in the success of the new laissez-faire would be a reduction in the power of organised labour and a general enlargement of social inequalities as part of the process through which the disciplines and incentives of the market were permitted to operate more freely; while the success of the new interventionism would entail, rather, a transfer of the power of organised labour from the industrial into the political sphere, accompanied by the legal and institutional consolidation of this power and by economic and social policies aimed at further advancing working-class interests' (ibid. p. 82).

It is possible that the conflict may go unresolved, as we slip into a 'twilight life of Keynesianism' in an effort to avoid serious conflict: 'if . . . the viability of radical alternatives is rendered problematic by the balance of power and advantage prevailing between opposing classes, most western nations may forego the possibility of pursuing them as the price that must be paid for social peace' (ibid. pp. 83–4).

6.7   A PROGRAMME FOR ECONOMIC RESEARCH

At present, the raw materials used by economic analysts and forecasters consist of series of statistics produced by governments and other institutions. Elaborate models are constructed that purport to determine the future consequences of movements in these series. Superficially, this seems similar to blind flying, when a pilot lands his aircraft in fog. There is, however, an important difference in that the pilot knows what it is that the instruments are measuring, and the instruments perform their functions with precision. Not so the statistical instruments employed in econometrics. Aggregates and general averages are not real economic phenomena. They do not act and react with or against each other, for the action takes place at the micro level between elements of which the statistical entities are abstractions (see Hayek, above p. 103). Identical averages in different periods may be composed of micro-phenomena that differ significantly, and it is these micro-phenomena that have to be identified, studied and observed.

For example, consumption must be studied by questioning consumers, detecting changes in patterns of consumption and seeking the reasons for the changes (see Katona and Strumpel, 1978). Movements in investment, employment, prices and incomes must be identified and explained not by manipulating statistical series but by the identification and interrogation of those who make the decisions that lie behind the statistics.

I know that knowledge is an impediment to speculation. There is great resistance to the proposition that the economic imagination should be curbed by the rigours of empirical research. Many and varied are the objections that are raised:

Our courses are not adapted for the contemplation of the real world. Then we must adapt them.

But such investigations require great skill. Then we must train the investigators.

But companies will refuse to answer our questions. Then we must persuade them. In fact, businessmen are not unco-operative: they are more often surprised and pleased when economists take the trouble to consult them.

But econometrics is about the specification and measurement of functional relations between statistical series. Asking the decision-makers is regarded as cheating. Then econometricians will have to change their ways.

This may not enable us to solve our problems, but at least we shall be able to understand them.

Summary

In Chapter 1, I listed seven different ways of viewing unemployment, each with strong political implications, and suggested the sort of methodology that enabled contrary views to co-exist. There followed a definition of unemployment, a note on various ways of measuring it, and a table showing the resulting statistics for unemployment (as defined) in various industrialised countries. We noted how rates varied between the principal OECD countries, highest in 1984 in the United Kingdom, lowest in Canada, Sweden and Japan. By September or October 1985 it had fallen a bit in Sweden and the United States, but in general there had been little change. Nowhere had it reached the proportions of 1932 and 1933, but it has proved to be much more persistent and refused to go away. In the 1930s, prosperity was restored by preparations for war; in present-day United States by a budget deficit likely to be $210 billion for 1984–5, between 5 and 6 per cent of GDP. In the United Kingdom the deficit for 1984–5 will be between 2½ and 3 per cent of GDP. Both governments are monetarists, but Mr Reagan is a pragmatic monetarist and Mrs Thatcher a dogmatic monetarist. We noted six facets of unemployment or ways of classifying the unemployed: by occupation, industry, region, age, sex, and duration. Like any mixture, unemployment varies in accordance with the changing proportions of its ingredients. The chapter ended with a classification of unemployment according to its causes: cyclical, seasonal, structural, technological, regional, frictional.

Chapter 2 was devoted to a history of unemployment, noting that the breakdown of feudalism and advent of capitalism had seen the appearance of an army of cottagers, paupers and vagrants, their numbers swollen or reduced by the business cycles to which capitalism was prone. We examined structural and technological unemployment, and ended by trying to distinguish one from another in the United Kingdom of the past thirty years. We found it not easy to do.

In Chapter 3 we examined what and how theorists had thought

about unemployment from the time of Sir William Petty (1623–87) to John Maynard Keynes (1883–1946). I suggested that it was possible to discern two lines of descent, one leading to the Welfare State, with human behaviour viewed as a product of social and psychological forces, the other to the market economy, with economic man subordinate to the urge for pecuniary gain. I argued that two sides were as distinct in their methodology as in their theory. The 'economic men' used the *a priori* deductive method, beginning with axioms and deducing, step by step, what would follow. The other lot were empirical and historical, seeking their material in studies of human behaviour and attrubuting importance to historic change rather than eternal economic laws. But Keynes was an exception: he was a proponent (indeed, the chief proponent) of the welfare state and simultaneously, at least until 1936, employed the *a priori* deductive method. Indeed, it was this identity of method that enabled his opponents to incorporate his theorems into their own mosaics, and led Beveridge to exclaim, 'The distinguishing mark of economic science, as illustrated by this debate, is that it is a science in which verification of generalisations by reference to facts is neglected as irrelevant' (Beveridge, 1937, p. 465).

Chapter 3 left economic thought at the end of the 1930s; Chapter 4 picks it up again towards the end of the 1950s, the subjects of contention now demarcated by Friedman and Phillips. The types of theory listed in Chapter 1 were demonstrated. When seen together, they constitute a confusion of ideas that I suggested you should test as you go along by asking of the theorist, 'How do you know? Are your findings based on the identification and study of those who make the economic decisions? Or are they plucked from the air?' I went on to expound Phillips's and Friedman's ideas, followed by those of two present-day monetarists. Then we pursued the course of contemporary debate: is there a natural rate of unemployment? does involuntary unemployment really exist? can economic decisions be deduced from the assumption of rational expectations? is there a trade-off between inflation and unemployment? could flexible wage rates clear the market? Then we asked, do trade unions cause unemployment and, if so, what can be done about it? Then we reviewed the arguments of those who believe in the improvability of the present system: the possibility that the contending parties might cure social ills by process of mutual accomodation. Doubt persisted, for few contributors had Professor Meade's faith in the persuasive power of common sense. The chapter ended with an outline of ideas from those who believed that a struggle was imminent in which someone was bound to get hurt, and would resist accordingly.

In Chapter 5 we evaluated the theories examined in Chapter 4, noting the aversion of most of the theorists to 'systematic empirical inquiry', and the remoteness of their models from practical significance. Supply-side economics, search unemployment, rational expectations and the natural rate of unemployment were found to be essays in the absurd. There are contradictory views of the responsibility of trade unions for unemployment. I asserted that 'managers are not helpless victims of circumstance over which they have no control', and that incomes policies are unlikely to succeed, even though the results of pay bargaining have been ludicrous.

Chapter 6 looked at options and possibilities for the future, my thesis: that capitalism's tendency to periodic mass unemployment is inherent in its decision-making process. Feedback augments its operative forces so that 'unreasonable hopes and unreasonable fears' become reasonable as soon as enough people share them. There are palliatives that can be applied, though their effects are complicated. Plans to adapt the system are considered: co-determination, workers' control, employee investment funds; neo-corporatism and other devices for mutual accomodation. There is a likelihood of stalemate, a possibility of radical change. But there are historical imperatives, connected with Britain's concern for the rest of the world, that will compel certain courses of action, with the development of Britain's scientific and cultural resources as the alternative to relapse into the status of underdeveloped country, a choice that will be politically determined. A programme for economic research is appended in terms of which economics would at last become operational.

Bibliography

Addison, John T. and Siebert, W. Stanley (1979) *The Market for Labor: an Analytical Treatment* (Santa Monica: Goodyear).

Aldcroft, Derek H. (1984) *Full Employment: the Elusive Goal* (Brighton: Wheatsheaf Books).

Andrews, P. W. S. (1949) *Manufacturing Business* (London: Macmillan).

—————— and Wilson, T. (eds) (1951) *Oxford Studies in the Price Mechanism* (Oxford University Press).

Armengaud, André (1970) *Population in Europe 1700–1914* (London: Fontana).

Artis, M. J. (1976) 'Is there a wage equation?', University College of Swansea and University of Manchester mimeo.

Association of Professional, Executive and Computer Staff (1979) *Office Technology: The Trade Union Response* (London: APEX).

—————— (1980) *Automation and the Office Worker* (London: APEX).

Atkinson, A. B. (1982) 'Unemployment, Wages and Government Policy', *Economic Journal*.

Bagehot, Walter (1873) *Lombard Street, A Description of the Money Market*. (London: Henry S. King).

—————— (1880). *Economic Studies* (London: Longmans, Green).

Bain, George Sayers (1966) 'The Growth of White-Collar Unionism in Great Britain', *British Journal of Industrial Relations*.

—————— (ed.) (1983). *Industrial Relations in Britain* (Oxford: Blackwell).

Ball, R. J. and Doyle, Peter (eds) (1969) *Inflation* (Harmondsworth: Penguin Books).

Barrett Brown, Michael (ed.) (1978) *Full Employment* (Nottingham: Spokesman).

Bauer, P. T. (Lord) (1984) *Reality and Rhetoric* (London: Weidenfeld & Nicolson).

Bell, Daniel and Kristol, Irving (eds) (1981) *The Crisis in Economic Theory* (New York: Basic Books).

Bennett, John (1984) 'Bibliography 1982', *British Journal of Industrial Relations*.

Berle, Adolf A. and Means, Gardiner C. (1935) *The Modern Corporation and Private Property* (New York: Macmillan).

Beveridge, William (1937) 'The Place of the Social Sciences in Human Knowledge', *Politica*.

——————, Lord (1960) *Full Employment in a Free Society* 2nd Ed. (London, Allen & Unwin).

Blackaby, Frank (ed.) (1980) *The Future of Pay Bargaining* (London: Heinemann).

Blaug, Mark (1980) *The Methodology of Economics* (Cambridge University Press).

Brittan, Samuel (1982) *How to End the 'Monetarist' Controversy* (London: Institute of Economic Affairs).

Brown, A. J. (1985) *World Inflation Since 1950* (Cambridge University Press).

Brown, William (1978) 'Social Determinants of Pay', *Working Paper No. 24* (Flinders, Australia: National Institute of Labour).

Bureau of Labor Statistics (1966) *Handbook of Methods for Surveys and Studies*. Bulletin 1458 (Washington: Government Printing Office).

Bythell, Duncan (1969) *The Handloom Weavers* (Cambridge University Press).

Campbell, R. H. and Skinner, A. S. (1982) *Adam Smith* (London: Croom Helm).

Central Statistical Office (1979) *Standard Industrial Classification*. (London: HMSO).

——— (1984) *United Kingdom National Accounts 1984 Edition* (London: HMSO).

Challen, D. W., Hagger, A. J. and Hardwick, P. (1984) *Unemployment and Inflation in the United Kingdom, an Introduction to Macroeconomics* (London & New York: Longman).

Clark, Colin (1981) 'Do Trade Unions Raise Wages?', *Journal of Economic Affairs*.

Clark, J. B. (1899) *The Distribution of Wealth* Reprinted 1956, (New York: Kelley).

Clarke, Tom and Clements, Laurie (1977) *Trade Unions under Capitalism* (Glasgow: Fontana/Collins).

Clower, R. W. (ed.) (1969) *Monetary Theory* (Harmondsworth: Penguin Books).

Cole, G. D. H. and Filson, A. W. (1951) *British Working Class Movements, Select Documents 1789–1875* (London: Macmillan).

Cole, Ken, Cameron, John and Edwards, Chris (1983) *Why Economists Disagree* (Harlow: Longman).

Coleman, D. C. (1983) 'Proto-Industrialization: A Concept Too Many', *The Economic History Review*.

Commission for the European Communities (1984) *The European Social Fund: Weapon against Unemployment* (Brussels: European File, 2/84).

Committee on Industry and Trade (1926) *Survey of Industrial Relations*. (London: HMSO).

Crouch, Colin and Pizzorno, A. (eds) (1978) *The Resurgence of Class Conflict in Western Europe since 1968* (London: Macmillan).

D'Avenant, Charles (1698) *Of the Public Revenues, and of the Trade of England*, reprinted in *The Political and Commercial Writings of that Celebrated Writer Charles D'Avenant*, Vol. 1 (Farnborough: Gregg Press, 1967).

Davis, Ralph (1973) *English Overseas Trade 1500–1700* (London: Macmillan).

Deane, Phyllis and Cole, W. A. (1969) *British Economic Growth 1688–1959* (Cambridge University Press).

Department of Employment (1971) *British Labour Statistics Historical Abstract 1886–1968* (London: HMSO).

Doeringer, Peter B. (1981) *Industrial Relations in International Perspective* (London: Macmillan).

Dutt, R. Palme (1947) *India To-Day* (Bombay: People's Publishing House).

Eden, Frederic Morton (Sir) (1797) *The State of the Poor: A History of the Labouring Classes in England* (3 vols) Abridged version, Rogers, A. G. L. (ed.), 1928 (London: Routledge).

Eichner, Alfred S. (ed.) (1983) *Why Economics is not yet a Science* (London: Macmillan).

Einzig, Paul (1952). *Inflation* (London: Chatto & Windus).

European Communities (1982) *Trade Unions in Denmark* (Brussels: EEC).

Feinstein, Charles H. (1976) *Statistical Tables of National Income, Expenditure and Output of the United Kingdom 1855–1965.* (Cambridge University Press).

Fogarty, Michael (1975) *The Just Wage* (Westport: Greenwood Press).

Ferguson, C. E. and Gould, J. P. (1975) *Micro-economic theory* (New York: Irwin).

Freedman, Robert (ed.) (1961) *Marx on Economics* (Harmondsworth: Penguin Books).

Friedman, Milton (1953) *Essays in Positive Economics* (Chicago: University of Chicago Press).

——— (1969) *Optimum Quantity of Money* (London: Macmillan).

——— (1977) 'Inflation and Unemployment', *Journal of Political Economy*.

Friedmann, Georges (1961) *The Anatomy of Work* (London: Heinemann).

Garraty, John A. (1978) *Unemployment in History. Economic Thought and Public Policy* (New York: Harper & Row).

Garside, W. R. (1980) *The Measurement of Unemployment. Methods and Sources in Great Britain 1850–1979* (Oxford: Basil Blackwell).

Glynn, Andrew and Harrison, John (1980) *The British Economic Disaster* (London: Pluto Press).

Godfrey, Martin (1985) *Global Employment: The New Challenge to Economic Theory* (Brighton: Wheatsheaf Books).

Goldthorpe, John H. (1983) 'Problems of Political Economy after the end of the Post-War Period', *Stato E Mercato*, no. 7, April. To appear also in Charles S. Maier (ed.) *Changing Boundaries of the Political* (New York: Cambridge University Press, forthcoming).

Gomes, Gustavo Maia (1982) 'Irrationality of "rational expectations"', *Journal of Post Keynesian Economics*.

Gordon, Robert J. (1982) 'Why US Wage and Employment Behaviour differs from that in Britain and Japan', *Economic Journal*.

Gourevitch, Peter *et al.* (1984) *Unions and Economic Crisis, Britain, West Germany and Sweden* (London: Allen & Unwin).

Hannington, Wal (1937) *The Problem of the Distressed Areas* (London: Victor Gollancz).

132   *Bibliography*

Hanson, Charles and Rathkey, Paul (1984) 'Industrial Democracy: A Post-Bullock Shopfloor View', *British Journal of Industrial Relations*.

Harris, José (1972) *Unemployment and Politics. A Study in English Social Policy 1886–1914* (Oxford: Clarendon Press).

Hayek, Friedrich A. (1935) *Prices and Production* (London: Routledge).

———— (1980) *1980s Unemployment and the Unions* Hobart Paper 87 (London: Institute of Economic Affairs).

Heilbroner, Robert L. (1972) *The Worldly Philosophers* (New York: Simon & Schuster).

Hepple, Bob (1983) 'Individual Labour Law', in George Sayers Bain (ed.) *Industrial Relations in Britain* (Oxford: Basil Blackwell).

Hicks, John (Sir) (1974) *The Crisis in Keynesian Economics* (Oxford: Basil Blackwell).

Higgs, Henry (ed.) (1959) Richard Cantillon *Essai sur la Nature du Commerce en Général* (London: Frank Cass).

Hobsbawm, E. J. and Rudé, George (1969) *Captain Swing* (London: Lawrence & Wishart).

Hobson, John Atkinson (1902 and 1938) *Imperialism, a Study* (London: Allen & Unwin).

———— (1896 and 1904) *The Problem of the Unemployed* (London: Methuen).

———— (1909) *The Industrial System, an Inquiry into Earned and Unearned Income* (London: Longmans).

———— (1922) *The Economics of Unemployment* (London: Allen & Unwin).

———— and Mummery, A. F. (1889) *The Physiology of Industry* (London: John Murray).

Holmes, George A. (1971) 'England: a Decisive Turning Point', in William B. Bowsky (ed.), *The Black Death. A Turning Point in History* (New York: Holt, Rinehard and Winston).

Houston, Rab and Snell, K. D. M. (1984) 'Proto-Industrialization? Cottage Industry, Social Change, and Industrial Revolution', *The Historical Journal*.

Hull, C. H. (ed.) (1899) *The Economic Writings of Sir William Petty*. (Cambridge University Press).

Hunter, L. C. (1980) 'The End of Full Employment', *British Journal of Industrial Relations*.

———— and Mulvey, C. (1981) *Economics of Wages and Labour* (London: Macmillan).

Hutchison, T. W. (1953) *A Review of Economic Doctrines 1870–1929* (Oxford: Clarendon Press).

ILO (1972) *Employment, Incomes and Equality* (Geneva: International Labour Office).

———— (1959) *The International Standardisation of Labour Statistics*. (Geneva: International Labour Office).

Inglis, Brian (1971) *Poverty and the Industrial Revolution* (London: Hodder & Stoughton).

International Industrial Relations Association (1983) *Collective Bargaining and Incomes Policies in a Stagflation Economy*, Conference report.

International Institute for Labour Studies (1984) 'Employment and

Unemployment: a continuing issue', Paper prepared for the Department of Studies of the Lutheran World Federation, Geneva.

Johnston, T. L. (1981) 'Sweden' in E. Owen Smith (ed.) *Trade Unions in the Developed Economies* (London: Croom Helm).

Joll, Caroline, McKenna, Chris, McNab, Robert and Shorey, John (1983) *Developments in Labour Market Analysis* (London: Allen & Unwin).

Kaldor, Nicholas (1972) 'The Irrelevance of Equilibrium Economics', *Economic Journal*.

Katona, George and Strumpel, Burkhard (1978) *A New Economic Era* (New York: Elsevier North-Holland).

Katouzian, Homa (1980) *Ideology and Method in Economics* (London: Macmillan).

Keynes, John Maynard (1930) *A Treatise on Money* (London: Macmillan).

———— (1933) *Essays in Biography* (London: Mercury Books).

———— (1936) *The General Theory of Employment, Interest and Money* (London: Macmillan).

Keynes, John Maynard and Henderson, Hubert (1929) *Can Lloyd George do it?* Reprinted in *The Collected Writings of John Maynard Keynes* IX *Essays in Persuasion* (London: Macmillan, 1972).

Knowles, K. G. J. C. and Winsten, C. B. (1959) 'Can the Level of Unemployment explain Changes in Wages?' *Bulletin of the Oxford University Institute of Statistics*.

Kornai, Janos (1971) *Anti-Equilibrium* (Amsterdam: North-Holland).

Layard, Richard (1981) *Unemployment in Britain: Causes and Cures* (London: Centre for Labour Economics, London School of Economics).

Lekachman, Robert (1967) *The Age of Keynes* (Harmondsworth: Penguin Books).

Leslie, Thomas Edward Cliffe (1888) *Essays in Political Economy* (Dublin: Hodges, Figgis).

Levy, S. Leon (1970) *Nassau W. Senior* (Newton Abbot: David & Charles).

Locke, John (1692) *Some Considerations of the Lowering of Interest and Raising the Value of Money. The Works of John Locke, vol. V*. Reprinted Aalen Scientifia Verlag, 1963.

Lucas, R. E. (1981) *Studies in Business-Cycle Theory* (Oxford: Basil Blackwell).

Maier, Charles S. (ed.) (1986) *Changing Boundaries of the Political* (Cambridge University Press).

Malinvaud, E. (1982) 'Wages and Unemployment', *Economic Journal*.

———— and Jean-Paul Fitoussi (eds) (1980) *Unemployment in Western Countries* (London: Macmillan).

Malthus, Thomas Robert (1836) *Principles of Political Economy* 2nd ed. (London: William Pickering) Reprinted by the International Economic Circle, Tokyo, and the London School of Economics, 1936.

Marcet, Jane Haldimand (1834) *John Hopkins's Notions of Political Economy* (London: Longmans).

———— (1851) *Rich and Poor* (London: Longmans).

Marsden, David (1978) *Industrial democracy and industrial control in West Germany, France and Great Britain* (London: Department of Employment).

Marshall, Alfred (1961) *Principles of Economics* 9th (Variorum) ed. (London: Macmillan).

Martineau, Harriet (1832) *Illustrations of Political Economy* (London: Charles Fox).

Marx, Karl (1887) *Capital* (Moscow: Foreign Languages Publishing House, 1961).

———— and Engels, Frederick (1848) *Manifesto of the Communist Party* (Peking: Foreign Languages Press, 1975).

Meade, James E. (1982) *Stagflation, Vol. 1, Wage Fixing* (London: Allen & Unwin).

Meidner, Rudolf (1978) *Employee Investment Funds. An Approach to Collective Capital Formation* (London: Allen & Unwin).

Mill, John Stuart (1844) *Essays on some unsettled questions of Political Economy* (London: Longmans) (Reprinted Clifton: Augustus M. Kelley, 1968 and 1974).

Miller, Robert and Wood, John B. (1982) *What Price Unemployment? An Alternative Approach* Hobart Paper 92 (London: Institute of Economic Affairs).

Minford, Patrick (1982) 'Trade Unions Destroy a Million Jobs', *Journal of Economic Affairs*.

Mitchell, B. R. and Deane, Phyllis (1962) *Abstract of British Historical Statistics* (Cambridge University Press).

Mitchell, Wesley Clair (1927) *Studies in Business Cycles, No. 1, The Problem and its Setting* (New York: National Bureau of Economic Research).

Moggridge, Donald (ed.) (1973) *The Collected Writings of John Maynard Keynes* Vol. XIV, *The General Theory and After* (London: Macmillan).

Myrdal, Hans-Göran (1980) 'The Swedish Model – will it survive?', *British Journal of Industrial Relations*.

National Economic Development Office (1984) *The Impact of advanced information systems on job boundaries* (London: NEDO).

Nickell, Stephen (1982, March) 'Wages and Unemployment: a General Framework', *Economic Journal*.

———— (1982, Sept.) 'The Determinants of Equilibrium Unemployment in Britain', *Economic Journal*.

OECD (1964) *International Joint Seminar on Geographical and Occupational Mobility of Manpower* (Paris: OECD).

———— (1965) *Wages and Labour Mobility* (Paris: OECD).

Office of Population Censuses and Surveys (1980) *Classification of Occupations* (London: HMSO).

———— (1982) *Census 1981, National Report Great Britain* (London: HMSO).

Ohlin, Bertil (1950) *The Problem of Employment Stabilization* (London: Geoffrey Cumberlege).

Owen Smith, Eric (ed.) (1981) *Trade Unions in Developed Economies* (London: Croom Helm).

———— (1983) *The West German Economy* (London: Croom Helm).

Parkin, Michael and Sumner, Michael T. (eds) (1972) *Incomes Policy and Inflation* (Manchester University Press).

Parry, J. H. (1968) *The European Reconnaissance* (New York: Harper & Row).

Pen, Jan (1963) 'The Strange Adventures of Dutch Wage Policy', *British Journal of Industrial Relations*.

Petty, William (Sir) (1899) 'A Treatise of Taxes and Contributions', in C. H. Hull (ed.), *The Economic Writings of Sir William Petty*. (Cambridge University Press).

Phelps Brown, E. H. (Sir) (1972) 'The Underdevelopment of Economics', *Economic Journal*.

Phillips, A. W. (1958) 'The Relation between Unemployment and the Rate of Change of Money Wage Rates in the United Kingdom, 1861–1957', *Economica*.

Pigou, A. C. (1933) *The Theory of Unemployment* (London: Macmillan).

The President [of the United States] (1979) *Employment and Training Report* (Washington: US Government Printing Office).

Reddaway, Brian (1959) 'Wage Flexibility and the Distribution of Labour', *Lloyd's Bank Review*.

Robinson, Derek and Mayhew, Ken (eds) (1983) *Pay Policies for the Future* (Oxford University Press).

Robinson, Joan (1962) *Economic Philosophy* (Harmondsworth: Penguin Books).

Rogers, James E. Thorold (1909) *Six Centuries of Work and Wages. The History of English Labour* (London: Swan Sonnenschein).

Roll, Eric (1973) *A History of Economic Thought* (London: Faber & Faber).

Rotwein, Eugène (ed.) (1955) *David Hume, Writings on Economics*. (Edinburgh: Nelson).

Rousseas, Stephen (1981) 'The poverty of wealth' in 'Symposium: Supply-side economics', *Journal of Post Keynesian Economics*.

Routh, Guy (1959) 'The Relation Between Unemployment and the Rate of Change of Money Wage Rates: A Comment', *Economica*.

———— (1974) 'Mobility of the Inhabitants of an English Town', *Growth and Change*.

———— (1975) *The Origin of Economic Ideas* (London: Macmillan).

———— (1980) *Occupation and Pay in Great Britain 1906–79* (London: Macmillan).

———— (1984) *Economics: an Alternative Text* (London: Macmillan).

Royal Commission (1834) *Report of His Majesty's Commissioners for Inquiring into the Administration and Practical Operation of the Poor Laws* (London: B. Fellows).

Samuelson, Paul A. (1964) *Economics, an Introductory Analysis* (New York: McGraw-Hill).

———— and Solow, R. M. (1960) 'Analytical Aspects of Anti-Inflation Policy', *The American Economic Review*.

Say, Jean Baptiste (1821) *Treatise on Political Economy* (London: Longmans).

Schienstock, G. (1981) 'Towards a Theory of Industrial Relations', *British Journal of Industrial Relations*.

Selwyn, Norman M. (1978) *Law of Employment* (London: Butterworths).

Senior, Nassau W. (1836) *An Outline of the Science of Political Economy* (Reprinted London: Allen & Unwin, 1938).
———— (1966) *Selected Writings on Economics* (New York: Augustus M. Kelley).
Showler, Brian and Sinfield, Adrian (1981) *The Workless State: Studies in Unemployment* (Oxford: Martin Robertson).
Sinfield, Adrian (1981) *What Unemployment Means* (Oxford: Martin Robertson).
Sismondi, Jean-Charles Léonard Simonde de (1819) *Nouveau Principes d'Économie Politique*, 2nd ed. 1827 (Paris: Calmann-Lévy, 1971).
Skidelsky, Robert (1983) *John Maynard Keynes, Hopes Betrayed 1883–1920* (London: Macmillan, 1983).
Smith, Adam (1776) *The Wealth of Nations.* Glasgow ed. of the *Works and Correspondence of Adam Smith* (Oxford: Clarendon Press, 1976).
Smith, Richard (1981) *Introducing New Technology into the Office* (London: Work Research Unit Occasional Paper 20).
———— and Quinlan, Terry (1982) 'Croydon Advertiser Group', *Meeting the Challenge of Change* (London: Work Research Unit).
Sraffa, Piero (ed.) (1962) *The Works and Correspondence of David Ricardo* (Cambridge University Press).
Standing, Guy (1981) 'The notion of voluntary unemployment', *International Labour Review*.
———— (1983) 'The notion of structural unemployment', *International Labour Review*.
———— (1984) 'The notion of technological unemployment', *International Labour Review*.
Stephenson, G. and Brotherton C. (1979) *Industrial Relations: A Social Psychological Approach* (Chichester: Wiley).
Streeck, Wolfgang (1981) 'Qualitative Demands and the Neo-Corporatist Manageability of Industrial Relations', *British Journal of Industrial Relations*.
TUC (1980) *Technological Change* (London: Trades Union Congress).
Turner, Michael (1980) *English Parliamentary Enclosure, Its Historical Geography and Economic History* (Folkstone: Dawson & Hamden, Archon Books).
Walker, E. Ronald (1943) *From Economic Theory to Policy* (University of Chicago Press).
Walras, Léon (1874) *Elements of Pure Economics* Translated by William Jaffé, (London: Allen & Unwin, 1954).
Warner, George Townsend (1924) *Landmarks in English Industrial History* (London: Blackie).
Webb, Sidney and Beatrice (1927) *English Local Government: English Poor Law History*, Part I. *The Old Poor Law* (London: Longmans, Green).
Whewell, William (1859) *Literary remains consisting of Lectures and Tracts on Political Economy of the late Rev. Richard Jones* (London: John Murray).
Whynes, David (ed.) (1984) *What is Political Economy?* (Oxford: Basil Blackwell).
Wicksell, Knut (1901) *Lectures on Political Economy* (London: Routledge & Kegan Paul).

Wiles, Peter and Routh, Guy (1984) *Economics in Disarray* (Oxford: Basil Blackwell).

Wilkinson, Ellen (1939) *The Town that was Murdered* (London: Victor Gollancz).

Willman, Paul (1982) *Fairness, Collective Bargaining, and Incomes Policy* (Oxford: Clarendon Press).

Wilson, Charles (1965) *England's Apprenticeship 1603–1763* (London: Longmans).

Worswick, G. D. N. (1984) 'The recovery in Britain in the 1930s', *Panel Paper No. 23* (London: Bank of England).

Wragg, Richard and Robertson, James (1976) 'Britain's Industrial Performance since the War', *Employment Gazette*.

Index